Writing the Second Act
Building Conflict and Tension in Your Film Script

Michael Halperin

"Halperin's brilliant research and revelations of the second act and its positive and negative effects on screenplays is a must-read for both new and mature writers. Most of the problems in screenplay writing occur in the composition of the middle act... a death trap for some writers and a bridge of brilliance for others. A must-read for theatrical writing."

Howard G. Minsky, Producer of *Love Story* and former theatrical agent with the William Morris Agency.

"You'd be amazed how many good writers have no technical understanding of why they write so well. Michael Halperin's gift is that he actually understands the mechanics of dynamic plotting, and *Writing The Second Act* will one day be regarded as the standard work on mid-story development. He cuts through all of the waffle, all of the mysticism and all of the pretentiousness and tells us in unnerving lucid terms why we're writing good stories. Or why we're not. If you want to be a success in movies, you'd better buy this book. And I don't even get a percentage."

Graham Masterton, Novelist and author of *The Chosen Child, Spirit, Black Angel* and more.

"*Writing The Second Act* is a rare combination - both a useful tool for screenwriters and a good read."

Peter Lefcourt, Television writer: *Daniel Steele's Fine Things, The Women of Windsor.* Novelist: *The Woody, The Deal, The Dreyfus Affair.*

"A must-have tool for beginning writers. A valuable reminder for professionals. I really enjoyed reading it so much I went back to rewrite some of my old scripts!"

Lynn Roth, Executive Producer of *The Paper Chase* for Showtime, and writer of multiple movies-of-the-week, including *The Patron Saint of Liars, A Bunny's Tale,* and *Babies.*

WRITING THE SECOND ACT
Building Conflict and Tension in your Film Script

Michael Halperin

Published by Michael Wiese Productions, 11288 Ventura Blvd. Suite 821, Studio City, CA 91604. (818) 379-8799 Fax (818) 986-3408.
E-Mail: mw@mwp.com
www.mwp.com

Cover Design by The Art Hotel
Interior Design and Layout by Susanne Manheimer Design
Printed by McNaughton & Gunn

Manufactured in the United States of America
Copyright ©2000 by Michael Haplerin.

Library of Congress Cataloging-in-Publication Data

Halperin, Michael
        Writing the Second Act: building conflict and tension in your film script/
        Michael Halperin.
        p.   cm.
        ISBN 0-941188-29-9
        1. Motion picture authorship. I. Title.
        PN 1996.H274 2000
        808.2'3--dc21

                                                        00-035200

DEDICATION

For Marcia who inspires me in all things.

WRITING THE SECOND ACT

BY MICHAEL HALPERIN

TABLE OF CONTENTS

INTRODUCTION ix

CHAPTER ONE:
In the Beginning 1

CHAPTER TWO:
Beginnings, Middles, and Ends 19

CHAPTER THREE:
Middles Not Muddles 51

CHAPTER FOUR:
Heroes and Villains 69

CHAPTER FIVE:
Enter the Hero 81

CHAPTER SIX:
The Big Battle 93

CHAPTER SEVEN:
Run for the Money 103

CHAPTER EIGHT:
The Big Race 117

CHAPTER NINE:
The Big Finish 127

CHAPTER TEN:
The Whole Story 141

REFERENCED FILMS AND THEIR WRITERS 155

THE WRITER'S LIBRARY 158

THE WEB 158

INTRODUCTION

The story of life has three distinct episodes: birth, life, and death – a beginning, a middle, and an end.

Birth and death arrive with pain, anguish, grief, sometimes terror, and sometimes with sublime peace. Life, on the other hand, has twists and turns along with complications and surprises. The second act always contains marvels and mysteries that astonish us, but all of which could have been prophesied if we had paid attention to the clues and milestones along the path.

Stories contain the same elements as life. They have beginnings, middles, and ends. The second act, the middle, holds the dynamic, dramatic and surprising conflicts and tensions introduced in the first act and resolved in the third act. And it happens to be the most difficult part of a screenplay or story to develop. The second act is the center of the story. It's the core that provides a sense of gravity firmly holding the screenplay together.

Over the years I have written for television and film, acted as story editor and story consultant at major studies and taught screenwriting to hundreds of university students at both undergraduate and graduate levels. The greatest challenge many writing students have – and a few writers who consider themselves professional – revolves around the development of the second act.

In my many sessions working with writers and students, I hear and read great openings or first acts and sometimes interesting endings or third acts. Then I ask the critical question: "So what happens in the middle?" Blank stares usually follow the question along with much hemming and hawing that end with statements such as "I'll figure it out" or "All kinds of things happen to the hero…"

That's why I decided to write a book about the second act. My hope is that it helps writers understand the importance of properly developing the struggle within the story as well as taking the characters to their breaking points before thrusting them into the third act resolution.

Chapter One
IN THE BEGINNING

For writers the second act represents a door opening, permitting us to lift our stories over a threshold and into a fascinating new world - where action, tension, conflict, romance, misery, comedy, and tragedy blossom and grow.

New writers or students engaged in writing courses often believe that all they need are exciting beginnings and rollicking conclusions. They have the mystical belief that a muse will emerge, sit on their shoulders, whisper magical incantations and the second act will write itself.

Unfortunately, life for writers does not exist in the same realm of fantasy as Albert Brooks' film *The Muse* (1999). Just as that character struggled to create and just as he realized that the "muse" must be fed, cared for, and nurtured, so do all creative efforts. Incredibly hard work - almost slavish labor - goes into the development of a screenplay.

A screenplay may be the closest prose form to poetry. Its spare, terse framework implies more often than it tells. It's designed to show the reader, the director, the cinematographer, the set designer, and the actors the story and the environment in which it takes place.

Anthony Minghella, the screenwriter of *The English Patient* (1997) and *The Talented Mr. Ripley* (1999) explained his view of the art of writing a screenplay: "Cinema is capable of poetry. If you can hand over to the director a map which has all of the territory properly corralled and choreographed, then the filmmaker can use this blue-print to create something whaich has its own poetry."[1]

---

[1] Susan Billington Katz. "A Conversation with Anthony Minghella." *Written By:* March 1997. Vol. 1, Issue 3, p. 22.

THE BASICS

Before concentrating on the second act, we need to journey through the basics. The three-act structure has existed since stories first were told. Greek tragedies, Elizabethan drama, modern plays, and screenplays all break down into three parts.

Without the setup in Act 1, the conflict in Act 2 cannot exist. And without the setup and conflict, the Act 3 resolution falls flat on its face.

Joseph Campbell clearly set out the triad of the mythic tale and life's pilgrimage in his "hero's journey" paradigm, when he divided ancient myths into three distinct parts.

Campbell's *Hero With a Thousand Faces* explores story construction in detail. Heroes (in this case they stand for males and females) leave their ordinary, mundane worlds and are enticed by, or voluntarily start out on, an adventure.

Before leaping into the adventure, heroes have to get past a presence that tries to prevent entry into the mystery. By defeating the presence – or guard – or whatever or whomever happens to hold the key to the door of the second act, heroes enter a strange, new world where large and small obstacles confront them.

The story enlarges with the addition of allies or associates who assist the heroes. Worthy adversaries attempt to thwart them from attaining their goals. Threats, tests, figurative and literal death, danger from all sides spring at heroes, who must face incredible ordeals in order to snatch the reward, thus proving that their journeys were proved worthwhile.

The "Hero's Journey" worked in 500 BCE and it ought to work today. Almost all of Alfred Hitchcock's films use this paradigm. In Ernest Lehman's screenplay *North by Northwest* (1959), Thornhill, (the character played by Cary Grant), a mild-mannered businessman, finds himself pushed from his ordinary world into the world of espionage. Thornhill becomes a hero by default, but once he enters the second act there's no holding back.

A mystery woman, played by Eva Marie Saint, is both helper and hindrance. Her character has similarities to mythic or legendary shape-shifters – those creatures who are allies and enemies, good and bad; whose motives sometimes seem benevolent and other times malevolent.

The paradigm also finds its way into comedies such as *The Full Monty* (1997) by Simon Beaufort. Garry and his friends come from the most mundane of ordinary worlds, the unemployed of Sheffield, England.

Out of work and out of cash, Garry faces the reality that his wife wants sole custody of their son. In the second act, he conceives the idea that he can make money by going "the full monty" – putting on a show in which he strips all the way.

The second act takes off because his chums and new friends join the venture. Some do it willingly, others reluctantly. During the course of the act, defections occur, setbacks loom, disappointments happen. They all come together in a motion picture that explores male bonding, male-female relationships, and the way in which individuals overcome economic and emotional adversity with humor.

OTHER PARADIGMS

While this paradigm is often effective with screenplays and has become increasingly popular with those who teach the craft, it certainly isn't the only one on which writers hang their stories.

In 1927, twenty-two years before Joseph Campbell wrote *The Hero With A Thousand Faces*, a Russian critic, Vladimir Propp, suggested that folktales could explain narrative structure. In *Morphology of the Folktale*, Propp set out the formula that Campbell may have adapted and expanded upon.

Propp's notion is that many stories begin with a difficult task proposed to the hero, who then forges ahead to accomplish the almost-impossible task.

A French critic, Claude Brémond, used Propp's formula, but suggested that as heroes move through the story they confront all sorts of trickery, temptation, or traps. Any time one or more of those obstacles pops up, the story can and will spin off in another direction.

Brémond's theory suits a complex narrative because it leads to multiple possibilities within a screenplay. Things go in and out of balance quickly - and that makes screenplays move.

Narrative structure can also proceed from the notion of "opposites," a concept formulated by the literary critic Tzvetan Todorov. In this structure, positives come up against negatives. "A" wants something and is thwarted by "B" who refuses to provide it or prevents "A" from getting it. "A" becomes driven to get what he/she can't have.

The classic thriller *Topkapi* (1964), written by Monja Danishewsky from the Eric Ambler novel *The Light of Day*, is one of the prime examples of this kind of narrative structure. The film has evolved into the model for many thrillers, including the motion picture reincarnation of *Mission Impossible* (1998) and *Mission Impossible 2* (2000).

Topkapi relates the story of the theft of a jeweled dagger from a museum fortress. The museum has apparently impregnable defenses which tempt the thieves into the adventure.

In the paradigm of opposites, the hero – often an anti-hero – drives forward as the result of an inner compulsion arising from the character's past. The back-story may be woven through the screenplay to make the character a fully realized person.

THREE CARDINAL ELEMENTS

Before beginning any form of writing, whether it's a screenplay, novel, short story or play, we need to lay down a firm foundation.

Analogous to blueprints, a solid foundation supports the structure, concept, and vision of a motion picture.

Unless the pieces fit together creating a strong framework, the work can break apart. Neophytes as well as professional writers often fall into the trap of believing they can create stories on the fly.

Sitting at the computer or scratching away on a legal pad and permitting the creative juices to flow may work for some creative geniuses. For the majority of writers, the lack of a firm foundation can lead to a sump of disappointment, lassitude, or that conveniently indefinite phrase "writer's block."

Writer's block usually comes about because no plan exists. When no plan exists we may flail about, searching for the right road to take us through our stories. If signposts do not appear at the crossroads, then it becomes tempting to push the pages away and go on to the next project, which may prove as abortive as the previous one.

The three cardinal elements we should concentrate on developing before plunging into our work are:
- •Focus
- •Logic
- •Character

KEEPING FOCUS

For the story to hold together, our characters and the way they function need focus.

It makes little difference whether the construction of our stories is linear, non-linear, or parallel. Maintaining a strong focus and firm hand will make writing a much easier process than if it's done by the seat of our pants.

Focus involves a number of considerations: Who are the characters?

Understanding the underlying drive behind characters provides them with a center of gravity. It keeps them planted firmly on the ground staked out by the writer. Without that knowledge, characters can float away from the story and dissipate the energy required to make it work.

When we know who and what our characters are about, if we comprehend all the possibilities inherent in them, then the way they grow not only surprises viewers, but makes sense to them as well.

Anthony Minghella is one of those writers who views characters as the reason for creating stories. "I'm most spurred on by the curiosity of what it means to be human. If the character is so distant from anybody that we know or understand, it's very hard to learn anything... I want to feel in film. I want to understand..."[2]

No one wants to hit the audience over the head with a heavily weighted psychological sledgehammer. On the other hand, intimate knowledge of the psychological makeup of characters can assist us in maintaining the consistency of their personalities.

[2] Richard Stayton. "The Talented Mr. Minghella." *Written By:* Feb. 2000. Vol. 4, Issue 2, p. 35.

Every story, whether it's a tale of love or an epic adventure, ought to have a goal. If, at the end of the screenplay, we don't have the foggiest idea of what the script accomplished, then it has failed.

Successful stories usually have a moral attached to them: "A penny saved is a penny earned"; "beauty is in the eye of the beholder," etc. Goals need not be lofty. They can be as simple as finding a soul mate, or as grand as forging peace on an intergalactic scale.

MAINTAINING LOGIC

When we develop a story with all of its characters, themes, and place, we engage in an act of creation.

It's just as much an act of creation as the biblical story of Adam and Eve in the Garden of Eden. In a way, when we write, we take on god-like attributes permitting us to form new characters, new worlds, and the rules by which those worlds operate.

What kind of world is it? It could be the mundane world of the ordinary – the one in which we live. We know the rules that operate here on Earth. Or it could be a world in the distant void of space where strange creatures leap and burrow, breed and war with one another.

It could be the extraordinary universe of *Star Wars* or the domestic neighborhood of *Ordinary People*. No matter what kind of worlds we create, they each operate within their own frame of reference – with their own logic.

If the law of gravity on Earth were repealed, everyone and everything not rooted to the surface would fly off into space. The same holds true for stories. That doesn't mean worlds that work by odd rules and peculiar laws, many of which would defy physics, can't be created. Of course they can.

Imagine, for example, a planet spinning in space in a galaxy far from the Milky Way. It has far greater gravity than Earth. On that planet live a mother and father who have just had a baby. The planet is about to explode and become a hail of planetary dust.

Those parents want to save their child so they wrap him in a blanket, place him in a small spaceship and send him on his way toward a distant blue planet, while behind him his home disappears in a fiery explosion.

When the child reaches Earth he has extraordinary powers. Since he came from a planet with a stronger gravitational field, this child can leap and bound much the same way astronauts bounced around on our own moon. The child can "leap tall buildings in a single bound." The story works because the writer set the rules – the frame of reference by which the entire story operates from that point on. Thus *Superman* came into being.

In *The Silence of the Lambs* (1991) screenplay by Ted Tally from the novel by Thomas Harris, everything the audience needs to know initially about the world they're going to enter appears on the first pages in a dramatically visual sequence.

INT. FBI ACADEMY — QUANTICO, VIRGINIA — DAY

CLARICE STARLING approaches us briskly down a long corridor. Trim, very pretty, mid-20s. She wears a grey "FBI Academy" sweatshirt, an ID badge, a navy ball cap. There are grass stains on the knees of her khakis, grass and sweat stains on her shirt. She reaches a closed door, stops, a bit flushed.

A NAME PLATE

there reads "BEHAVIORAL SCIENCE/Special Agent Crawford."

CLARICE

pulls off her cap, then doesn't know where to put it. She takes a deep breath, knocks on the door. No response.

                                        CUT TO:

INT. CRAWFORD'S OFFICE — DAY

Clarice opens the door, steps hesitantly inside. There is no one there. She looks around the office curiously, seeing it for the first time.

HER POV

A cramped and obsessively cluttered room. Case
file materials — police and lab reports, manila
folders, photos — are stacked mountainously high
on the desk, the floor, the chairs. On the
walls: maps, charts, and screaming newspaper
headlines ("Buffalo Bill Claims 5th Victim,"
"FBI: Still No Leads on Buffalo Bill"). Most
prominent of all is a row of five enlarged
black-and-white photos — the faces of young
women, taken from life.

CLARICE

steps further into the room, staring at a BLACK-
BOARD filled with feverishly scrawled notes:
"Big women only… Skinning=Hunter?
Trapper?… Lunar cycle? No."[3]

In a few well-chosen words Tally conveys feelings, emotions, and a
gut-wrenching vision of brutality.

The very first page of the screenplay gives the reader a sense of that
particular world. Since Clarice attends the FBI Academy, we know
she's in the process of becoming an agent.

Her nervousness and fumbling become more apparent as the screenplay unfolds. But it's not innocence the writer conveys. It's a certain
naivete buttressed by an inner strength. Those characteristics evolve
so that they play in contrast to her adversaries.

---

[3] Ted Tally. *Silence of the Lambs.* All excerpts by permission of the author.

Once Clarice enters the office she finds herself confronted by a barrage of sensory information. The visuals show viewers and readers the kind of case in which Clarice may soon become involved. The eerieness of the headlines and the visual punch of the photos, along with the scrawled comments on the blackboard, all add up to a frame of reference that tells us we're on our way into the mouth of hell. It also becomes a warning to Clarice that the door opening before her should remain closed.

When her supervisor, Crawford, appears and announces only minutes later that she's been elected to interview the one person who may know the identity of the killer, Tally has prepared the reader/audience to unconsciously accept the notion of "Hannibal the Cannibal."

From that point on, the writer maintains the frame of reference - or the logic of the piece - and by so doing, pulls the reader/audience into a strange surrealistic world.

If we set the frame and then break it, viewers will react to the fractured logic by disconnecting from the story, thereby losing any momentum we may have generated.

We have to think of that frame in the same way science views the law of gravity, action versus reaction, and the speed of light. They are constants within the world of the characters' emotional turmoil.

DEVELOPING CHARACTER

The best screenplays, novels, plays, and short stories have characters that propel the story forward. They become the story and their power makes it work.

A Comedy of Language

In *Shakespeare in Love*, written by Marc Norman and Tom Stoppard, Will Shakespeare suffers from "writer's block" and attempts to forget his craft while pursuing the seemingly unattainable Viola.

Viola, promised in marriage to a nobleman she does not love, pursues her desire to act on the stage in Elizabethan England. It's an ambition destined to be thwarted since the law makes it illegal for women to appear on stage.

Once in disguise and onstage with young Will, she falls as much in love with him as he is in love with her. According to the fanciful screenplay their love story becomes the catalyst for the writing of *Romeo and Juliet*.

Norman and Stoppard set up the characters ingeniously. Shakespeare, young, nervous, worried about whether he will ever fill a page again and constantly ripped off by his producers, seems ripe for venting his romantic imagination.

Viola, despising her situation in life, finds love in the arms of the youthful Shakespeare. However, she knows she will never be able to marry him since her father has betrothed her, and she is beholden to obey. Her realization that it cannot work heightens when she discovers that Will left a wife, Anne Hathaway, back home with his children.

Both characters, as well as the secondary ones, have fully fleshed lives that affect the story and the way in which all the characters interact.

A Drama of the Mind

Paul Schrader's adaptation of Russell Banks' novel, *Affliction*, delves deep into the dysfunctional pasts of several characters.

At first we wonder why Wade Whitehouse rages and appears self-destructive. His girlfriend, aptly named Margie Fogg, at first doesn't see him for what he is. He must lose her as well as the love of his young daughter before he can attempt to come to terms with himself.

As the story progresses, Wade's father, Glenn, intrudes in his life. A man who hates women and drinks to excess, he pushes his son as hard as he can to make Wade hate him. It is a hatred that began early in life.

The "Affliction" of the title represents the passing of an emotionally crippled life through the Whitehouse family from generation to generation.

The exploration of this multigenerational attitude hits home. Even though our own family may not seem as bad as the Whitehouses, we all have secrets in our own lives that have an impact on the way we treat others and the manner in which we view our own lives.

Too often, writers tend to create stories and then place their characters aboard them like passengers on a train. The characters travel with the screenplay, rather than fuel the engine that drives the story forward.

The Drama of Creation

The creation of fully fleshed characters – whether they are human or alien – requires in-depth knowledge of their personalities and their psychological underpinnings. No character ever arises fully developed from the dust of earth.

At the beginning of this chapter, I wrote somewhat grandiosely that writers are similar to gods because they create worlds and characters that never existed. While this may be true, every character has antecedents. Every character comes from somewhere; has either a mother or a father or both; perhaps has siblings; lives through trauma and pain; or enjoys the good life.

Joys, sorrows, uplifting experiences, tragedies, flaws, and relationships give characters a unique perspective in order to excite and engage the audience. Unless those who populate our screenplays come off as real people - or creatures - we could find it increasingly difficult to maintain a connection with our stories, or with those to whom we tell our stories.

We have to go beyond the two-dimensional by burrowing beneath the skin of our creations. Films only stand up when we populate them with well-rounded characters, whether good or bad, whether protagonists or antagonists.

Knowing Our Characters

The first question we have to ask ourselves about our characters is how and why do they react to the situations we set up for them? By developing their life stories, we can answer that question.

All characters come from someplace and are going somewhere during the course of the story. They had a life prior to the tale, and, we presume, will have a life long after - unless we kill them off or they pass on to their great reward before the end credits roll.

The screenplay doesn't represent the totality of their existence. Once "The End" appears on screen the audience should feel the characters have completed only one part of their journey. It's up to us as writers to provide audiences with enough information so they can imagine what the future holds.

When screenplays become a series of coincidences, and characters act and react out of convenience to plots, they can become turgid and boring. Reason and logic dictated by the framework we establish should remain consistent.

Normal worlds ought to work by familiar rules. Other realms should operate according to the rules we create. We have to adhere to those rules, or the story will not make sense.

Characters ought to have purpose, and every scene must have its own drive based on what occurred before. Plot devices and character arcs that happen without foreshadowing divert audiences and hurt the story.

The drive behind stories should come from within the characters and the situations in which they find themselves. We should not impose it as the result of momentary whim or by the nature of forces outside the screenplay's frame of reference.

PUTTING IT ALL TOGETHER

Before tackling the daunting task of creating the second act - where all conflict, tension, battles, obstacles, enemies and allies exist - it's necessary to understand the basic elements that form the substance of all good stories.

Maintain focus by concentrating on the main thrust of the story and the characters. Understand the purpose of the story and the protagonist's and antagonist's goals.

Maintain the logic of characters and story by retaining the frame of reference – the rules of the world we create. Those rules may be strange, odd, realistic, or surrealistic. But once established, they ought to remain consistent.

Develop characters who have a history and a sense of place. All characters have origins that affect the way they act and react to situations. They may change as the story progresses, but those changes should be consonant with who the characters are and where they come from.

EXERCISES:

View videotape of *Silence of the Lambs*.

1. Identify where Act 1 ends and Act 2 begins.

2. Describe the story twist that indicates the move into Act 2.

3. Explain what makes that scene effective.

4. Describe Clarice Starling's principal goal.

5. Identify the subtext (underlying aim) of *Silence of the Lambs*.

6. Literal and Figurative Threats:

       A. Describe the literal threat to Clarice.
       B. Describe the figurative threat to Clarice.
       C. Relate how the two threats unite in the story.

Chapter Two
BEGINNINGS, MIDDLES, AND ENDS

When I review scripts with new writers I often hear the same mantra: "I want to write something new. Something with a new feeling. Something with a new way of telling a story. I don't want to follow the same old rules of screenplay writing or story telling." I admire that kind of adventurous soul. I want to promote and promulgate the creative forces behind such passion.

We all know the old saw that rules are made to be broken. However, we have to *know* the rules before we can smash them. That's why it becomes important to understand structure prior to taking it apart.

Look at the illustration of a painting titled "Science and Charity" on page 20. It depicts an ill woman with a doctor at her side. A nun holds her child while the doctor takes the woman's pulse. It appears to be a genre painting of the late 19th century. The artist knew how to paint figures. He understood light and shadow and perspective. Most of us would be hard pressed to guess the name of the man who painted it. He became one of the great modern masters of the 20th century. His name: Pablo Picasso. Before he became an abstract painter best known for the deconstructionist style called Cubism, Picasso understood the rules of painting.

The same holds true for writing. The three-act structure has existed since humans first found their voice. Storytellers understood that tales with beginnings, middles, and ends enthralled their listeners.

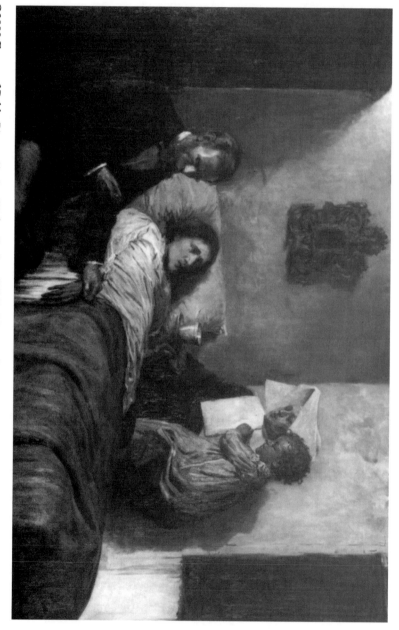

ELEMENTS OF ACT 1

What is the story about? What is the oncoming conflict? From where does the conflict originate? These questions ought to be answered - or at least explored - in the first part of the screenplay.

In the previous chapter we saw how Ted Tally established the environment - i.e., the mise-en-scène and the coming conflict for *Silence of the Lambs*.

The dark, dour opening of his screenplay prepares the audience for a ride through a horrifying, harrowing story. In a way, it's easier to set up the conflict when it's a battle between absolute evil and good.

In the screenplay *The Sweet Hereafter* (1997) written by Atom Egoyan from a novel by Russell Banks, the journey becomes more problematic due to the deliberate ambiguity into which the writer draws us. Who is innocent and who is guilty?

The simple story upon which everything rests involves an accident. A school bus skids off a highway and sinks beneath an ice-covered pond, killing almost all the children aboard. Mitchell Stephens, a personal injury attorney, represents the parents of the children on the bus. He plans on suing the bus company for negligence.

The children bring home the problem Mitchell has with his own daughter. His personal tragedy becomes interwoven with that of the families he faces in the remote snow-covered village where the accident occurred.

The first act introduces Mitchell and the difficulty he has with his drug-addicted daughter, Zoe. Initially he comes off as a father who wishes to divest himself of his child. Then we see his genuine anguish.

He arrives in the village and contacts the parents of the children who were killed and injured. The screenplay moves back and forth in time, creating within the audience a sense of foreboding as to what actually happened the day the bus crashed through the ice.

Discussing his screenplay, Egoyan said: "...the structure of a film is a question of preparing the viewer for what they need to receive and understand in terms of the underlying psychology of what's happening to these people."[4]

We meet Mitchell on the first pages of the screenplay. As he moves through a car wash, his cell phone rings. It's his daughter, Zoe.

```
INT. CAR WASH — NIGHT
                    MITCHELL
     Nothing's wrong with trying to talk
     to me, Zoe.


                    ZOE
               (over the phone)
     So what's the problem?
```

---

[4] Susan Billington Katz. "A Conversation with Atom Egoyan." *Written By:* Feb. 1998. Vol. 2, Issue 2, p. 27.

MITCHELL
The problem is I have no idea who
I'm talking to right now.

ZOE
(over the phone)
'Cause you think I'm stoned, Daddy?
Is that what you're thinking, Daddy?

Pause. Mitchell doesn't respond.

INT. PHONE BOOTH — NIGHT

ZOE
Are you wondering if I scored, Daddy,
and I'm calling you for money? That
I'm begging? God, I don't fucking
believe it!

INT. CAR WASH — NIGHT

Mitchell is emotionally stunned by Zoe's voice.
She is heard over the phone.

ZOE
(over the phone)
Daddy! Are you listening to me,
Daddy?

The music that Mitchell has been listening to
becomes louder as he stares at the spinning felt
wheels of the car wash.

                    ZOE
        DADDY!

                  MITCHELL
        Yes.

                    ZOE
        Why can't you talk to me?

                  MITCHELL
        I... I just need to know what state
        you're in so I know... how to talk to you...
        how to act...

Mitchell is in pain. He closes his eyes.[5]

With a strong, emotional immediacy the problem burning within
Mitchell erupts and becomes the leitmotif throughout the screenplay. It has the effect of bringing home the tragedy for the parents
of the children in the school bus accident.

It also raises questions about Mitchell. Is he heartless and cruel to
his own daughter? Or is he a broken man because of the disappointment he feels as a result of his daughter's addiction? And the most
important question of all: what happened between father and daugh-

---

[5] Atom Egoyan. *The Sweet Hereafter.* ©1997, Ego Arts Films. All excerpts used with permission.

ter to push her into a life on the streets?

The short scene played over a cell phone and a public telephone also creates the sense that there remains a tie, however tenuous, between Mitchell and Zoe.

The tension that exists between them comes home in another scene juxtaposed with Mitchell's arrival in the small Canadian town.

Mitchell, flying toward his rendezvous with the parents of the dead and injured children, finds himself sitting next to an old friend of Zoe.

```
A young woman seated beside Mitchell hands him
her headset.
                    ALISON
        You can have mine.


Mitchell takes ALISON'S HEADSET.   Their eyes
lock for a moment.

                    ALISON
        Yes, we do know each other.   I'm
        Alison Jones.


                    MITCHELL
        Alison Jones.
```

                    ALISON
I was a friend of Zoe's. We went to
school together. I used to come to
your house.

                    MITCHELL
        (pretending to remember)
Yes.

                    ALISON
Ally. That was my nickname.

                    MITCHELL
Ally. That's right.

                    ALISON
How are you?

                    MITCHELL
I'm just fine, Ally. What about you?

                    ALISON
I'm fine. Still working with my
father.

                    MITCHELL
And what does he do again?

                    ALISON
        He used to work with you.

Pause. Mitchell finally remembers Alison Jones.
                    MITCHELL
        Alison.

                    ALISON
        How is Mrs. Stephens?

                    MITCHELL
        We're… not together.

                    ALISON
        I'd heard that. But she's well?

                    MITCHELL
        Yes… fine.

                    ALISON
        And Zoe? How's Zoe?

Pause. The stewardess comes back with a new
HEADSET. She notices the set that Alison gave
him.
                    STEWARDESS
        Oh, you've beaten me to it.

The stewardess hands the headset to Alison.

> STEWARDESS
>
> Here.

The camera has remained fixed on Mitchell's face.

A chance encounter cracks a window open through which the audience learns a secret. The difficulties Mitchell has in dealing with his own problems and the difficulty he has in dealing with Zoe begin to emerge in Act 1.

At the end of the act, the other side of the story develops. It deals with the accident and the attitudes of the people Mitchell wishes to represent.

The audience feels the pain of the parents as represented by the Ottos. Mitchell's professional personality emerges, but is infused with his own story.

INT. THE OTTOS' HOUSE — DAY

Mitchell walks in the OTTO residence. It is a large two-story space divided into several smaller chambers with sheets of brightly colored cloth — tie-dyes and Indian madras — that hang from wires.

On a low brick platform in the center of the main chamber is a large wood-burning stove. A few feet from the stove, sitting on an overstuffed cushion, is Hartley Otto.

Hartley is listening to music on his headphones.
He is very stoned. Wanda moves over, and pulls
the headphones off her husband's head.

                    WANDA
     We have a guest. What did you say your
     name was?

                    MITCHELL
     Mitchell Stephens.

Mitchell hands them a card. Hartley reads it
with deliberation.

                    WANDA
     The Walkers sent him by.

Hartley rises up. He stares at Mitchell. A
tense pause.

                    HARTLEY
     You want a cup of tea or something?

                    MITCHELL
     A cup of tea would be nice.
                    (Beat)
     Would it be alright if I sit down

for a few minutes, Mrs. Otto?   I
want to talk to you.

Wanda stares at Mitchell.   No response. Mitchell
waits a beat, then seats himself rather uncom-
fortably on a large pillow.   He is unsure of
whether to cross his legs, or fold them under
his chin.

                    MITCHELL
    The Walkers spoke very highly of you.

                    WANDA
    You've been retained?

                    MITCHELL
    Yes.

                    WANDA
    Their child died, and they got a lawyer.

Pause.   Mitchell assesses Wanda's energy.

                    MITCHELL
    It should be said that my task is to
    represent the Walkers only in their
    anger.   Not their grief.

                    WANDA
    Who did they get for that?

                    MITCHELL
You are angry, aren't you Mrs. Otto?
That's why I'm here. To give your
anger a voice. To be your weapon
against whoever caused that bus to
go off the road.

                    WANDA
Dolores?

                    MITCHELL
It's my belief that Dolores was doing
exactly what she'd been doing for years.
Besides, the school board's insurance
on Dolores is minimal. A few million at
the very most. The really deep pockets
are to be found in the town, or in the
company that made the bus.

                    WANDA
You think someone else caused the accident?

                    MITCHELL
Mrs. Otto, there is no such thing as an
accident. The word doesn't mean anything
to me. As far as I'm concerned, somebody
somewhere made a decision to cut a corner.
Some corrupt agency or corporation account-
ed the cost variance between a ten-cent

```
bolt and a million-dollar out-of-court set-
tlement. They decided to sacrifice a few
lives for the difference.  That's what's
done, Mrs. Otto.  I've seen it happen so
many times before.
```

By the end of *The Sweet Hereafter's* first act, the audience understands part of the conflict that will blossom in the second act. The conflict that exists between Mitchell and his inner doubts and demons parallels the discord about the accident bubbling beneath the surface within the community.

At the same time, secrets abound in the tightly knit community. Secrets they would just as soon ignore and pretend do not exist.

The writer sets up a surprising twist in the story. The sole survivor of the accident, Nicole, has an incestuous relationship with her father, Sam. Eventually that relationship tears down Mitchell's case and brings home the ties to his daughter, Zoe.

Egoyan believes secrets are at the heart of his adaptation. "...It's what's most provocative to me about the theme in this story. It's a clash between legal - some would say moral - narrative, personal narrative and communal narrative. What holds a community together? It's a shared history. And yet certain histories have been deprived or denied."[6]

---

[6]Todd Lippy. "Writing and Directing *The Sweet Hereafter*: A Talk with Atom Egoyan." *Scenario: The Magazine of Screenwriting Art.* Winter 1997. Vol. 3, No. 4, p. 42.

ELEMENTS OF ACT 2

In order to keep interest moving, the second act usually begins by rolling off a twist at the end of Act 1.

Now the hard work begins. Stories live or die by the development of major conflicts as well as the interrelationships of characters.

Our protagonists must cope with an evolving situation. It doesn't matter if we write drama, comedy, or adventure. Somewhere along the line some kind of disaster looms ready to thrust the story forward.

It could be the Titanic hitting an iceberg, or apparitions rising out of the sewers of New York to wreak havoc on its population. It might be a giant mega-bookstore ready to overtake the small mom- and-pop shop around the corner. Or it could be something as personal as two people in love who have different cultures or secrets that keep them apart.

The situation builds emotional levels to a fever pitch. Our characters may face incredible obstacles. They may fall in love. War may be declared. They may seek revenge.

Within this buildup of heightened anxiety, awareness, comedy, or danger, our protagonists ought to look at the world they have entered and ask: "How did I get into this?" This forward motion brings us inevitably toward the resolution of the story or the problem.

Before we reach that point, we have to ask ourselves whether or not we care about the people we created. If we don't care, the story will not hold together.

The second act should reveal the emotional, passionate, funny, or diabolical edge of the story. Whatever we attempt in the screenplay must end up satisfying the audience.

The Sweet Hereafter picks up its pace in Act 2. The characters introduced in the first act begin to reveal themselves. It turns out more is going on in the small town than Mitchell realizes.

Nicole, who ends up as the sole survivor of the bus accident, recites Browning's "The Pied Piper of Hamelin" to Billy's children. That scene plays in counterpoint to the crash and the children's death. At the moment of the accident, Billy tails the bus in his pickup truck while waving at his children who watch him through the rear window.

In an earlier scene with the children, Mason, Billy's young son, questions Nicole about the Pied Piper in a way that foreshadows coming events, but also provides insight into why Nicole eventually destroys Mitchell's lawsuit.

                    MASON

       Nicole?

                    NICOLE

       Yes?

                    34

                    MASON
Can I sit beside you on the bus
tomorrow?

                    NICOLE
Don't you usually like to sit at the
back? To wave at your Dad.

                    MASON
I want to sit beside you tomorrow.

                    NICOLE
Okay.

Nicole covers Jessica and gets up to leave.

                    MASON
Nicole?

                    NICOLE
What, Mason?

                    MASON
Did the Pied Piper take the children
away because he was mad that the
town didn't pay him?

                    NICOLE
That's right.

                              MASON
          Well, if he knew magic — if he could get
          the kids into the mountain — why couldn't
          he use his pipe to make the people pay
          him for getting rid of the rats?

                              NICOLE
          Because… he wanted them to be punished.

The scene above intercuts with scenes of an adulterous affair between Billy and Risa who, along with her husband Wendell, owns the motel in which Mitchell stays during his investigation.

Following the consummation of Billy and Risa's most recent tryst, the screenplay moves to Nicole and her father Sam engaging in their incestuous relationship. Nicole numbs the moment by continuing to recite "The Pied Piper of Hamelin" to herself, in which she finds kinship with the one last child who was too lame to follow the piper.

The metaphor is not hard to grasp. Her friends died on the bus and Nicole was left behind in a wheelchair. She can't understand how she survived, and as a result feels enormous guilt. At the same time she must continue to endure her father's advances.

While Mitchell has no knowledge of any of this, the death of the children brings back the memory of his own daughter, Zoe, who almost died at the age of three from the bite of a Black Widow spider. The scene of Zoe's childhood plays in counterpoint to the scene of the accident.

The end of Act 2 comes fast when Nicole realizes that her sister, Mary, may be next in line for her father's unwanted sexual attention. That scene plays against a flashback in which Mitchell receives a phone call from his daughter and discovers that she has tested positive for HIV.

Mitchell must make his choices while Nicole makes a decision that changes the course of events for everyone. This surprise pulls us into the third act. Now we have a need to learn the resolution of the various stories intertwined in *The Sweet Hereafter*.

Egoyan follows the dictum of the great writer-director Billy Wilder, who states that: "...the second-act curtain launches the end of the picture... but not just the end. You'd better have another twist in the third act... You expect that it's all over. No. Now comes the end."[7]

ELEMENTS OF ACT 3

Whatever conflict we create rises to a peak at the end of Act 2 and takes us toward the resolution. The audience ought to feel satisfied with that resolution. The conclusion we develop must appear to be the only one that works.

With all the possible twists and turns our characters take during the life of the story – while gleaming on the flickering screen for that brief moment – they continue to live in the imagination. Where are they going and how will they get there?

[7] Cameron Crowe. "Conversation with Billy." *Vanity Fair.* Oct. 1999. No. 470, p. 313.

Those questions can only be answered by providing the audience with satisfying information about the men, women, and children we create. The information we present must make sense in terms of how we set up the characters, who they are, how they live, and how they face the vicissitudes created for them.

The conclusion and resolution may express themselves in new knowledge about the characters' development. Death may bring a new dimension to the story. Revelation of an event or an interior part of the characters usually plays a large part in the third act.

Conflicts must resolve themselves, plots must be reconciled, and relationships may continue beyond the end of the screenplay. In order to accomplish that in the viewers' eyes, we have to develop impetus – forward motion – so that the audience has a notion of how the characters will continue to live out their lives.

The example used in this chapter, Egoyan's *The Sweet Hereafter*, gives us an opportunity to visualize an unusual screenplay that accomplishes this task.

First, the writer surprises us when Nicole testifies in her deposition that the accident was no one's fault. With that startling revelation Mitchell's case starts to unzip.

Nicole's character begins a voiceover narration that slips in and out of the scenes as if she's viewing it from a great distance.

Her description takes hold of us, and we realize that she deliberately lies in order to undo everything that preceded this moment. She defies her father, Sam, who looks at the accident as a way of collecting big money from the bus company.

Mitchell sees it as a way of continuing his career, and as a way of rectifying the wreck that is his daughter's life. The ties that hold the town together unravel one string at a time. It becomes apparent that Nicole wreaks vengeance on her father - and in so doing takes revenge on the entire town for not protecting her and the other children. The final sequences of the screenplay explore the future. They take place after the depositions and after the case has dwindled away.

```
EXT. AIRPORT — MORNING

At the airport, in the arrivals bay, Mitchell
waits for his limousine.

Across the road, a hotel minibus is parked.  The
driver is Dolores.  The camera settles on her
face as she stares at Mitchell.

Mitchell catches her gaze, and the two stare at
each other.

                    NICOLE
                (voice over)
        As you see each other, almost two
        years later, I wonder if you realize
```

something.

Mitchell's limo arrives. He gets inside.

INT. LIMOUSINE — MORNING

CLOSE-UP of Mitchell as he stares ahead, lost in thought.

                    NICOLE
                (voice over)
    I wonder if you realize that all of
    us — Dolores, me, the children who
    survived, the children who didn't —
    that we're all citizens of a different
    town now.

EXT. GAS STATION — DAY

Billy watches as a crane lifts the demolished school bus onto a flatbed truck.

                    NICOLE
                (voice over)
    A town of people living in the sweet
    hereafter.

EXT. CAR — AFTERNOON

Nicole and Sam driving home from the fairground.

> NICOLE
> (voice over)
> "Where waters gushed and fruit trees grew and everything was strange and new."

The camera leaves the car to look up at the sky.

EXT. FAIRGROUND - DUSK

Sunday night at the fairground. Nicole is staring at the Ferris wheel. In her imagination, the swinging cars of the slowly turning wheel are full of children. The laughter and noise is haunting.

Nicole smiles as she stares at this private apparition.

INT. BILLY'S HOUSE - JESSICA AND MASON'S BEDROOM - NIGHT

Nicole has just finished reading a story to Jessica and Mason. The children are asleep. Nicole puts the book down, and kisses the two sleeping children on the cheek.

```
Nicole gets up to leave the bedroom, leaving the
door slightly open.

Light spills in from the hallway.
```

The screenplay concludes with a scene that plays throughout the story. It also gives us a vision of Nicole as she is and as she was - remaining a tragic, wheelchair-bound character who has finally taken control of her own life.

Mitchell's case turns into a disaster, but he will move on to the next one and the one after that - still pursuing the daughter he has lost. He will continue his attempt to bring her back, but without the slightest idea of how to accomplish it.

In his own way, Mitchell's character moves in what may be viewed as a downward spiral, paralleled by his daughter's descent into the netherworld of drugs.

The audience has seen not only a resolution to the immediate conflict of the story, but also recognizes that some elements of the screenplay have not been tied up neatly with ribbons. At the same time, we have an inkling of where the characters are going and what their inevitable fates may be.

ACT CONSTRUCTION

The opportunity to establish the major units of construction for our screenplays occurs in Act 1. It prepares us, as writers, and the audience for looming conflict that hurtles us into exciting adventures, love stories, horror tales, or science-fiction epics.

Act 2 develops from the setup we create in Act 1. Motivations established for the characters become refined and redefined. The main elements of conflict and tension heighten. We reveal, moment-by-moment, the anxieties, needs, wants, and desires of protagonists and antagonists.

The story evolves as the plot takes our characters into dead ends; as they face dilemmas; as they come face to face with their own failings and shortcomings; and as they encounter their own demons and angels.

Characters find themselves involved in situations from which they must climb, creep, or crawl. When they extricate themselves from one situation they may find themselves embroiled in another.

Whether the screenplay is *The Sweet Hereafter*, or *Shakespeare in Love*, or *Affliction*, Act 2 ratchets up the excitement generated by Act 1.

Where and how and with whom the conflict and tension evolve is, of course, up to us. Suffice it to say that unless those elements exist and make sense within the context of the universe that we establish at the outset, the story will dissipate and disappear as we search for a door leading to the conclusion.

Near the culmination of Act 2, stories and characters usually have a moment of revelation when things become clear. That moment thrusts us into the third act.

The conclusion of the story and its resolution usually find expression in new information about the characters and the story. Whatever we learn in Act 3 has to remain consistent with how the story and its characters have been set up in the previous two acts.

Yes, we want to surprise the audience. On the other hand, we do not want to introduce foreign elements into the screenplay that have no relevance to anything written up to that point. Surprises ought to be kept within the context of how we create our characters and stories. Switching things at the last moment because the idea happens to intrigue us only confuses audiences and disrupts the flow.

If the idea happens to be one we cannot live without, then we have to return to the previous acts and foreshadow our intent. Forshadowing does not telegraph meaning. It only provides clues – subtle clues for the most part - as to what may happen in the future. Then when the foreshadowed event does occur, the audience will still react with surprise, yet also with an understanding of why the action, the scene, or the sequence played out as it did.

Often the understanding occurs on a subliminal level. For example, in *The Sweet Hereafter* the story of the "Pied Piper of Hamelin" supplies clues for the third act resolution.

Reconciliation of plots and relationships are further refined in Act 3. This does not mean that we must wrap up all threads of the story. While the main plot may resolve itself, smaller, life-affirming, dangerous, or quirky plot lines may be left to the audience's imagination. On the other hand, we have the responsibility to ensure that the audience has an inkling of where those plot lines may be heading.

Characters continue living after the final credits appear on screen. Therefore, we ought to give the audience a glimpse into the future in order to assure them that they have a handle on possible outcomes.

The careful crafting of characters in the first act, with its initial invitation to the coming conflict or tension in Act 2, represents only the tip of the iceberg. We introduce our characters, but not in their entirety. Act 2 explores them in depth, drawing the audience into their psyches.

The same holds true for story development. We use Act 1 to furnish clues, foreshadow events, provide impressions, and create a sense of forward movement. Act 2 begins the process of answering questions posed in Act 1.

CONFLICT

The basic conflicts or common themes in most screenplays, novels and plays are "People vs. People," "People vs. Nature," or "Person vs. Self." Screenplays that mirror those conflicts resonate with audiences. They often deal with topics such as love, war, or sex.

Very few stories, however, link themselves directly to a single theme. Usually they are a mixture of several themes, with one overriding all the others. In *The Sweet Hereafter* Egoyan skillfully weaves the legal battle fought by the parents against the corporation, Nicole and her terrible secret, and the story of Mitchell and his inner battle. Each is a metaphor for the other.

This represents only the beginning and the setup for conflict. This setup establishes the tension that exists between or within characters, and the external and internal pressures exerting forces on them.

EXTERNAL PRESSURE

External pressures are those that come from outside the character. They are the influences over which characters have little or no control.

The majority of films directed by Alfred Hitchcock fall into this category. In *North By Northwest*, the main character finds himself mistaken for a mysterious man who has something of value the antagonists want. The heavies kidnap him and he must use his wits to escape the dilemma.

An excellent example of external pressure occurs in *Three Days of the Condor* (1975), screenplay by Lorenzo Semple, Jr. and David Rayfiel from the novel *Seven Days of the Condor* by James Grady.

Iconoclastic Joseph Turner works at the American Literary Historical Society, in actuality a CIA front. He reviews books to determine if they reveal codes used by foreign powers to pass secrets back and forth.

Turner leaves his office for a few minutes. In that short time, assassins invade the facility, brutally massacring everyone in the building. When Turner returns he discovers the bloodbath and goes on the run, fearing they will come after him as well.

Although a CIA front employs him, he works in a benign position. Outside forces are determined to kill Turner because they suspect he may reveal the inner workings of a diabolical scheme run by a rogue organization within the Central Intelligence Agency.

Once again, the protagonist finds himself thrown into an unforeseen predicament, where he must use intelligence and skill to extricate himself.

INTERNAL PRESSURE

Internal pressures are those that come from within characters. Usually they have to do with faults or cracks in the protagonists' psyche or mental makeup.

The 1996 film *Spitfire Grill*, written by Lee David Zlotoff, uses the characters, Percy and Hannah, who appear as opposites, to demonstrate how each represents a mirror image of the other. Angst brought about by internal pressure fills each woman with her own doubts and fears.

Although the original predicament in which Percy found herself – in prison for manslaughter - came about as the result of another person, she needs to rid herself of internal demons that have pursued her ever since.

Hannah, an irascible old woman who claims to need no one, faces her own demons by shielding her battle-traumatized Vietnam veteran son, whom she claims died in battle, from the small community.

Eventually, the internal dramas of these two women collide. When they do, it forces them to build an uncomfortable alliance that affects the small Maine village of Gilead. It's a not-too-subtle reference to the hymn, "There is a Balm in Gilead," indicating that healing must begin in order to achieve a restoration of peace, even if sacrifices must be made.

PUTTING IT ALL TOGETHER

Most experienced screenwriters rarely make a conscious effort to create all the elements that go into the first act. However, when we read successful screenplays, we realize that these elements usually have found their way onto the page.

Major Themes

Establishing the major theme or themes of a story at the outset makes the development of the second act much easier. Those themes help generate the conflict to come. They also aid us in creating the tension that must exist in all stories. Without tension, screenplays would read as dull, plodding stories.

Protagonist/Antagonist

Act 1 also introduces protagonists and antagonists. While we should not lay everything on the line and reveal everything about the characters at this point, we ought to provide enough information for the audience so they have an idea of who the characters are and what motivates them.

Foreshadowing

Along with information about the characters, we should introduce relevant clues so that when they show up in Act 2 or Act 3 the audience is not taken unawares. Surprise without foreshadowing – even subtle foreshadowing – leads audiences to wonder about the intent. Without hints and clues, the story may crumble.

External/Internal Pressure

External pressure forces our characters to enter strange or unfamiliar realms. Through their intelligence, strength, wit, humor, or even by obtaining a magic amulet, they eventually overcome their problems and emerge from the tale with some kind of victory.

Internal pressure boils up within our characters - forcing them to face their inner demons and exorcise them before a catharsis takes place. Once the specters are defeated, change usually takes place within the characters, and also within the environment occupied by the characters.

49

The pieces of the puzzle may not appear to fit together initially, but by the end of the act they will move closer together, gathering the impetus that drives the screenplay into the third act.

EXERCISES:

Break down your own screenplay or work of fiction.

1. Describe briefly each of the acts.

> **A.** Identify the breaks between Acts 1 (setup), 2 (conflict and tension), and 3 (resolution).
> **B.** Demonstrate how the twists at the end of Acts 1 and 2 force the viewer to want to continue.

2. Describe the surprises or unexpected moments in each act.

3. Explain how you foreshadow those moments.

4. Examine the conflict(s) in your story. How is it expressed?

5. Identify whether this is a story of external pressure or internal pressure. Describe how the characters and story reveal the pressure exerted on them.

Chapter Three
MIDDLES NOT MUDDLES

Act 2 represents the heart of the screenplay. The true beat and flow of blood pulses here. The tension of muscle and sinew takes place here. Passions rise and fall and emotions grab our characters, forcing them into places and situations they never thought of, nor ever expected to find.

Once we create the basics of characterization in Act 1, the next step is to flesh out our characters in such a way that audiences will connect with them. That does not necessarily mean viewers will identify *with* the characters. They can revile them, be revolted by them, hate them, or pity them. Of course, identification *with* protagonists can only help the story.

Identification has to do with certain characteristics, not wholesale affinity. The hero who goes up against the establishment reminds us all of those times when we fought the telephone company in order to get an extension in our home. The character who battles nature in the form of a marauding grizzly or a devastating tornado reminds us of our own battle when an earthquake cracked our walls or torrential rain washed away our favorite garden.

By extension we understand the nature of heroism and why characters become heroes. According to the Campbell paradigm, heroes who come from the ordinary world are pushed into the role reluctantly.

The Todorov paradigm of "opposites" takes another tack. Heroes or anti-heroes want something that appears out of their reach, and they take action to get it.

With either structure, audiences understand a character's prime motivation for entering the story. Many of us have found ourselves dropped into a situation not of our own making and have had to swim hard to get out of it and resolve the dilemma.

Some of us have faced situations where a desired goal appears just out of our reach and we strive to reach it. Our own goals and desires may not have the heightened excitement of a *Raiders of the Lost Ark* or *Star Wars: The Phantom Menace,* or even the modest goal of falling in love with a motion picture star and winning her, as in *Notting Hill.* On the other hand, we have all aspired to achieve goals that, to us, are just as important.

MAINTAINING INTEREST

Screenplays should entertain, enthrall, and excite audiences. They can entrance, elicit curiosity, and make viewers feel good about themselves and the world in which they live.

It's true that an exciting premise gets us into a story. Some of us may not find it a challenge to create an exciting or endearing ending. The challenge arises when we have to maintain momentum while developing the conflict that leads to that ending. The story must move forward so that our protagonist or protagonists continually cope with an evolving situation.

Whether we write comedy, drama, or adventure, somewhere within the second act some kind of disaster looms. Foreshadowing the disaster keeps the audience guessing: When will it happen? What will happen to the characters? How will they get out of the situation? Will the lovers come together?

Countless successful screenplays have built themselves upon these premises. A meteor slams into Earth. Lovers agree to meet atop the Empire State Building on New Year's Day and miss one another. Unforeseen dangers lurk behind the cloning of dinosaurs.

Each inciting situation has the promise of building emotional levels to a fever pitch. Our characters may face incredible obstacles. They may fall in love, which may or may not turn out to be a barrier to their happiness. War may be declared. They may seek revenge.

STRUCTURING ACT 2

Some authors of "how-to" books on screenwriting emphasize the use of a set group of beats that ought to occur in each act.

Strict obedience to those rules may make it seem as if writers create screenplays in the same way an amateur hobbyist paints by the numbers. The results may satisfy the paintbrush wielder, but the paintings will all look alike.

While I do not favor rigid adherence to specific rules, some suggestions may assist in triggering new ideas and ways of handling scenes and sequences.

One of the best examples of a screenplay with an apparent three-act structure is *The Third Man*, written by Graham Greene based on his own story. Although produced in 1949 in the aftermath of World War II, the structure and story remain as solid today as when the film was first released. Greene's screenplay, adhered to scrupulously by the director Carol Reed, is a classic textbook for anyone wishing to write for the cinema.

Briefly, the story concerns Holly Martins, a starving writer of western pulp fiction, who comes to post-war Vienna in order to work for a charity founded by his old college friend, Harry Lime.

On his arrival, he discovers that Harry died in an unfortunate accident. His burial takes place at that very moment. A small group of acquaintances attends the funeral. They include a young woman, Anna Schmidt, who was Harry's lover, and two mysterious Austrians, Baron Kurtz and Dr. Winkel.

One other person hovering at the edge of the funeral is Lt. Calloway, a member of British security. He tells Holly that Harry was implicated in a sordid blackmarket ring dealing in diluted penicillin.

Holly now has a mission: to clear Harry's name of this infamous accusation. During his investigation, he learns that two men were on the scene when the accident occurred. However, the plot takes a turn at the end of Act 1 when a witness, the porter in Harry's building, informs Holly that more than two men were on the scene. There was a third man.

This becomes the leaping-off point as the screenplay shifts into fourth gear, taking us into Act 2. The story rolls forward like an unstoppable truck hurtling down a steep highway with no brakes.

The Third Man is told from Holly's point of view. Since he's a naive individual who doesn't speak German, whenever anyone speaks the language it isn't translated, thus placing the audience in Holly's shoes.

By the end of Act 1 Holly has met with Baron Kurtz, who insists that Calloway's accusations are ill-founded. The Baron tells Holly that Harry's last words were concern for him.

Holly also meets Anna, an actress, who takes him to Harry's apartment - where the Porter reveals information that seems at odds with the Baron's story.

> MARTINS
> Could he have been conscious?

> PORTER
> Conscious? Cas soll ich auch
> noch wissen?

> MARTINS
> Oh, er — was he — was he still
> alive?

                    PORTER
          Alive?   He couldn't have been
          alive, not with his head in the
          way it was.

                    MARTINS
          I was told that he did not die at
          once.

                    PORTER
          Er war gleich tot — I mean, sie
          war gleich tot — brauchen kein angst
          zu.   Ein moment… Wart ein bissel…
          Wartein bissel.   Fraulein Schmidt!

The Porter walks through the living room toward
the bedroom.   Martins follows after him.

                    PORTER
          Wis sagt men in English gleisch tot?

Anna combs her hair at the dressing table.

                    ANNA
          He was quite dead.

The Porter turns around looking for Martins,
then discovers him behind him.

                    PORTER
He was quite dead.

Anna looks in the mirror. She picks up an
unframed photograph of herself standing at the
open door of a car, waving. She puts the photograph in the drawer of the dressing table.

                    MARTINS
                    (O.S.)
But that sounds crazy. If he was
killed at once, how could he have
talked about me, and this lady here,
after he was dead? Why didn't you
say all this at the inquest?

The Porter walks to Martins.

                    PORTER
It is better not to be mixed up in
things like this.

                    MARTINS
Things like what?

                    PORTER
I was not the only one who did
not give evidence.

                    MARTINS
Who else?

                    PORTER
Three men helped to carry your
friend to the statue.

                    MARTINS
Kurtz.

                    PORTER
Yes.

                    MARTINS
The Roumanian?

                    PORTER
Yes.

                    MARTINS
And?

                    PORTER
There was a third man — he didn't
give evidence.

                    MARTINS
You don't mean that doctor?

PORTER

No, no. He came late after they
carried him to the Joseph statue.

MARTINS

What did this man look like?

PORTER

I didn't see his face. He didn't
look up. He was quite — gewernlich…
ordinary. He might have been…just
anybody.

Martins looks out the window.

MARTINS

Just anybody.[8]

At this point we can almost sense the curtain falling on Act 1 of *The
Third Man*. It provides us with an introduction to all the characters
critical to the screenplay. It also furnishes us with a foreshadowing
of events that become important to the interrelationships between
the characters and the revelations to come about them.

For example, as innocuous as it seems when first seen in the ceme-
tery, Baron Kurtz carries a small dog with him. That dog becomes a
small clue for Holly in order for him to understand the relationship
between the Baron and Dr. Winkel.

[8] Graham Greene. *The Third Man*. All excerpts by permission of the Graham Greene Trust.

Act 2 spins off the Porter's comment about "the third man." The Porter becomes angry with Holly. A small child sees the spat and runs off. That piece of action becomes an event that returns to haunt Holly.

Holly enters the twists and turns of the Viennese underground, the black market, and relationships between the various occupying powers. He also learns more and more about his old college chum, Harry Lime. Holly may have first suspected his friend of minimally illicit dealings, but revelation upon revelation seem to convincingly implicate Harry in a major blackmarket operation.

In the middle of Act 2, the writer creates a scene of terror that alternates with comedy, then slides into high-stakes danger.

Holly appears at the hotel looking for Calloway. When he can't locate him, he decides to take a taxi to Calloway's headquarters. Conveniently, a taxi waits at the door. It takes off like a bullet careening through the streets. Holly believes he's being kidnapped and set up for assassination. The car screeches to a halt and he's ushered in to a hall, where he's been expected as the guest speaker for a cultural evening.

The unexpected car ride and the fear that Holly exhibits come as a surprise to the audience. When it turns out not to be what we first suspected, we do not react as if the writer has duped us. Greene prepares the way earlier in Act 2 when the cultural attaché, Crabins, invites Holly to lecture at one of his forums. Again, Greene cleverly foreshadows the event.

Completely unprepared, Holly makes a fool of himself in front of the crowd. The light, almost comedic moment turns into life-threatening danger when one of the heavies appears with two goons. Holly runs for his life, evading the villains.

That sequence, the pursuit through the bombed-out wreckage of Vienna, becomes another foreshadowing of the climax of the motion picture - when Holly and the police will chase Harry through the vast underground sewers of the city.

ACT 2 BEATS: THE ROAD THROUGH THE MAZE

The beats in Act 2 of *The Third Man* make clear the rising tension and anxiety, and the twists and turns Greene creates in order to keep the audience focused on the story.

• The police take Anna in for questioning about Harry and his blackmarket dealings.

• Holly, playing the hero right out of one of his own western novels, attempts to come to her rescue.

• Anna's past is revealed when the police determine that her passport is forged. She's threatened with deportation back to the Russian sphere of influence; this raises the stakes for Holly.

• Holly visits Dr. Winkel to find out about "the third man." While there, the Baron's dog runs into the room, revealing a relationship between Winkel and the Baron.

• Holly, in his naive stance, reveals to the Baron that the Porter had seen "the third man."

• Anna and Holly's relationship becomes more and more entwined as Holly becomes infatuated with her.

• The Porter is murdered. The small child tells the crowd about the arguement he witnessed (see page 60) and the people assume Holly is the culprit. They pursue Holly (another foreshadowing of the chase in Act 3).

• Calloway attempts to prove to Holly that Harry was a true villain. He presents evidence demonstrating that Harry sold diluted penillin which caused the maiming and death of hundreds of people.

• Holly leaves Anna's apartment, only to discover Harry - watching him from the shadows. Harry disappears into the sewars.

• Calloway disinters the coffin in which Harry was supposed to be buried. He discovers the body of another person, a hospital orderly named Harbin.

• Anna is arrested and prepared for deportation.

• Holly arranges a meeting with Harry.
(See the graph of Act 2 of The Third Man on page 64).

Throughout the act, the writer provides clues to Harry Lime's psychological makeup, Holly Martins' personality, and Anna Schmidt's motivations. In a scene that takes place in Anna's apartment, Anna asks Holly to tell her something about Harry's life before she met him.

                    MARTINS

      Oh, we didn't make much sense.
      Drank too much. Once he tried
      to steal my girl.

                    ANNA

      Where is she?

Martins throws down the script and stands at the window.

                    MARTINS

      Oh, that was many years ago.

                    ANNA

      Tell me more.

                    MARTINS

      It's very difficult. You know
      Harry — we didn't do anything
      very amusing. He just made everything
      seem like such fun.

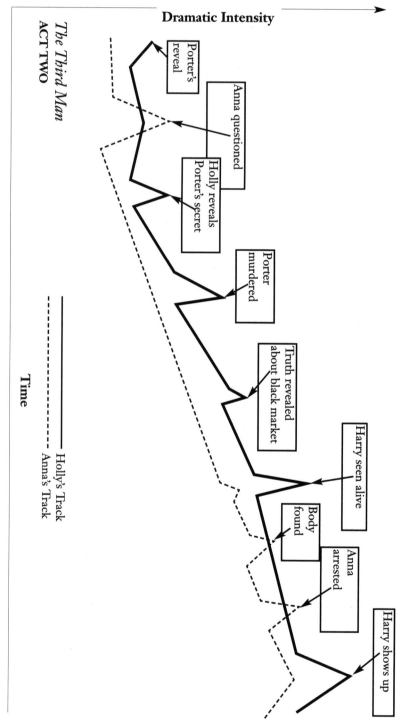

Dramatic Intensity

ACT TWO

The Third Man

Porter's reveal

Anna questioned

Holly reveals Porter's secret

Porter murdered

Truth revealed about black market

Harry seen alive

Body found

Anna arrested

Harry shows up

——— Holly's Track
--------- Anna's Track

Time

> MARTINS
> I suppose so. He could fix anything.

> ANNA
> What sort of things?

Martins strikes a match and lights a cigarette.

> MARTINS
> Little things. How to put your
> temperature up before an exam —
> the best cribs. How to avoid this
> and that.

In that brief exchange Graham Greene reveals that Harry has always been a scam artist. Once he had been the bad boy of their college days. Now it has translated into bigger vices.

Later, Holly expresses regret about trying to prove Harry's innocence. Because of his lack of sophistication he has stepped upon a path he should not have walked. He almost gives up until faced with his own sense of justice - a sense of justice we understand when he talks briefly about the kind of western novels he writes, in which good always conquers evil.

Anna's motivation for her loyalty to Harry emerges in a very brief line of dialogue when the authorities arrest her. They confiscate her love letters from Harry along with her passport.

Calloway holds her passport in his hand:

> CALLOWAY
> They'll be returned to you, Miss
> Schmidt, as soon as they've been

examined.

                ANNA
    There's nothing in them. Harry
    never did anything. Only one small
    thing once, out of kindness.

                CALLOWAY
    And what was that?

                ANNA
    You've got it in your hand.

Graham Greene does not waste a moment in the story. He provides hints, clues, and tips that subliminally prepare us for the coming action without making it obvious.

The excitement inherent in the story intensifies as a result of the interplay between the various characters. The principal protagonist drives the story forward. We find ourselves running in his shoes just as confused as Holly - as he attempts to deal with strangers in a foreign country - discovering hidden things that disrupt his deeply ingrained moral code, which by now we have adopted as our own.

PUTTING IT ALL TOGETHER

While the whole screenplay must carry the audience along with it, the second act has the principal purpose of holding the audience's interest.

By creating characters that cope with an ever-evolving situation, the audience remains with the story and the characters in order to discover how they will handle the predicament.

We have to ask ourselves several questions about Act 2 during and after writing the screenplay. At what point does the crisis begin to expand? What will happen to our character or characters when that happens? How will they extricate themselves from the developing events?

Increasing anxiety, awareness, comedy, or danger holds the audience to their seats and prepares them for the next revelation.

Heightening the risks for the protagonist during Act 2 also focuses audience interest. Risks do not mean only physical risks. Our stories may involve emotional risks, financial risks, or moral risks. Whatever they happen to be, it's important for the audience to identify with them and stay with our protagonists.

EXERCISES:

1. Examine your own screenplay or story, or view a video of an existing film, and outline the beats or story points that make up the second act.

2. Describe the clues provided in your screenplay or in the video that illuminate the story.

Chapter Four
HEROES AND VILLAINS

Heroes and villains – or protagonists and antagonists – usually show up in the first act where writers furnish their initial motivation for entering the battle.

That battle can be a war story or a love story. It can be written as an outrageous comedy or a sordid melodrama. It can soar through outer space or rumble through a ghetto.

Wherever it takes us, we understand that whoever our hero happens to be - man or woman - he or she needs a worthy antagonist. If not worthy, why bother with the battle?

Too often both professional and novice screenwriters present antagonists as devices for the protagonist to play against rather than as meaningful adversaries. When heavies have genuine motivations, they provide us with opportunities to develop conflict and tension that pulls the audience along with the story.

Conversely, when protagonists have good reasons for going up against meaningful black hats, stories can spin off in fascinating, dramatic directions, keeping audiences on the edges of their seats willing to suspend disbelief.

RAISING THE STAKES

The second act provides us with numerous possibilities for raising the stakes between hero and villain.

In the Campbell paradigm, unwilling heroes cross a threshold where they become active participants in attempting to solve a mystery or gain some kind of mystical, spiritual, or real reward. All sorts of obstacles cross their paths, including enemies (antagonists) whose aim is to prevent them from achieving their goals.

Unfortunately, when the paradigm becomes more important than story and character development, villains become mere set pieces who function only as obstacles for the benefit of the protagonists' heroics.

Campbell's *Myths, Dreams and Religion* goes beyond classic structure and examines more thoroughly the function of the enemy. It explores the purpose of villains as those who attempt to thwart heroes from accomplishing any tasks that have value for them or for society.

The chief villain in the biblical Exodus story is Pharaoh. Had he been someone who just wanted to stop Moses and the Israelites from leaving Egypt, the story would not have the effect it has had for almost 3000 years.

The recent animated film *Prince of Egypt* (1999) demonstrates that the tale continues to have meaning to people, young and old, even at the beginning of the 21st century.

Pharaoh's motivations come from his belief that he is a god on earth. When confronted by a new concept of a deity, he rebels. He cannot accept that this rag-tag gaggle of slaves and nomads who challenge the accepted worldview could destroy a way of life that has existed along the Nile for thousands of years.

He will protect his sovereignty, his land, his religion, and his people at all costs. Both Moses, as the hero of the story, and Pharaoh, as the villain, are heavily invested in achieving their goals. They are both "involved to the extent of their very interests."[9] Pharaoh's interests lie in the preservation of the monarchy and rule of the god-king.

[9] H. Frankfort. *The Intellectual Adventure of Ancient Man.* 1946. p. 7.

Moses' interests lie in an escape from slavery, the future and freedom of his people, and the right to worship their God without fear of oppression.

We can understand the motivation that exists for the antagonist and protagonist in this archetypal story. Because of the nature of the characters, each of them strong-willed and "stiff-necked," we want to see the outcome. Will might conquer or will right overcome?

This is drama and tragedy at their highest levels. Most screenplays written today do not involve God, the gods, pharaohs, or prophets. They deal with people mired in dramatic or melodramatic situations, humorous or farcical events, or action-adventure and fantasy episodes.

However, writers do use archetypes when developing their stories. James Cameron with Gale Anne Hurd created one of the most unlikely scenarios with *Terminator* (1984).

A child to be born in the 20th century will become the savior of the world in the 21st century. Forces in the future send an assassination machine back in time to destroy the mother before she gives birth.

Biblical archetypes for *Terminator* include the story of the Exodus in which Pharaoh orders the death of all the Israelite male children, and the story of Herod who orders the death of all Hebrew male children - one of whom is destined to become King of the Jews, Jesus.

Terminator's heroes, Sarah Conner and Kyle Reese, race against time and the future while being pursued by an agent of a futuristic pharaoh or Herod. The second act becomes a battle of intelligence against sheer malevolence and unstoppable computer power. Every few pages raise the ante.

In Act 2 we meet the real Sarah Conner watching a newscast of other Sarah Conners who have been systematically and viciously murdered. Although the audience has been introduced to her in Act 1 we know little about her.

Her first piece of action, an athletic leap over a bar in a saloon, gives us our first inkling of Sarah's strength and determination. A few pages later Sarah escapes from the Terminator even though it looks almost impossible.

Her wits save her life. It comes through loud and clear that this is one smart, spunky lady.

Near the end of Act 2, Reese reveals the secret of the future and the part Sarah will play in it as the mother of John Conner (note the initials: J.C.), the savior of a future world. We learn that Sarah will be the one who teaches her son to fight, organize, and prepare for the day when the forces of good and evil clash.

Although the assassination machine looks like a human being, he has only one motivation: to kill Sarah Conner. He cannot be deterred from that course. His programming will not change.

However, facets of his character do emerge throughout the second act. Aside from his implacable drive, he demonstrates a canny cleverness that surprises us.

He can change his voice. He can self-repair (shown in a scene where he peels back his false flesh and reveals to us that he is indeed a creature of metal, wires, diodes, and computer chips).

The Terminator is also a creature with a mission – one that can be understood by anyone who has lived in the 20th century and seen the genocidal actions of totalitarian governments. His mission: to prevent anything that will alter the future.

In the motion picture *In the Line of Fire* (1993) written by Jeff Maguire, Frank Horrigan is a Secret Service agent with a dark past. He was one of the men assigned to protect John Kennedy in Dallas in 1963. Ever since then he has battled his demons, wondering if he could have saved the President's life.

Given another opportunity thirty years later, Horrigan confronts an antagonist who knows his story, and uses it in an attempt to break him down.

This clever adversary calls himself "Booth" after John Wilkes Booth, the killer of Abraham Lincoln. Maguire uses Booth as his device for informing us about Frank's life. Booth's knowledge becomes a weapon for taunting the agent.

In the middle of the second act, the writer heightens the anxiety and tension between both men when Booth calls Frank at Secret Service headquarters:

```
EXT. WHITE HOUSE AND EXECUTIVE OFFICE BUILDING
— DAY

The White House glistens in the sun, the symbol
of the presidency, while over this we hear:


                    BOOTH
                 (voice over)
          Frank?  I hope you don't mind me
          calling you at the office.  I was
          in the neighborhood.
```

                    FRANK
                (voice over)
        No, why don't you drop by?

The phone call continues as we

CUT TO:

INT. SECRET SERVICE HEADQUARTERS — DAY

FRANK is on the phone, surrounded by AL and several other agents including

CARDUCCI and MAHER who sit before an array of
electronic and taping equipment, gesturing for
FRANK to keep Booth talking while they work to
trace the call.

                    BOOTH
                (on phone)
        I'd love to, Frank. Let me take some
        time to welcome those who are joining
        us late. I'd love to drop by. I'd
        like it a lot. We've got so much in
        common.

                    FRANK
        We do, huh? Like what?

                    BOOTH
        We're both willing to trade our
        life for the president. We're
        both honest, capable men who
        were betrayed by people we trusted.

                    74

> FRANK
> I wasn't betrayed, Booth.

> BOOTH
> Sure you were, Frank... The Warren
> Commission's report on the assassina-
> tion — They called your procedures
> "seriously deficient." They crit-;
> cized you and the other agents who
> were out drinking late the night
> before — As though Kennedy would
> be alive today had you been in bed at
> ten p.m. It's ludicrous —

Frank swallows hard, looks over to find Lilly
and Sam listening in on headphones.

> FRANK
> Maybe they were right.[10]

In that one scene, the writer reveals Horrigan's doubts, fears, and
anxieties. Later in the act, we discover Booth's motivations.

REVELATION IN STEPS

The information does not come in large expository statements.
Instead, the audience becomes privy to the secrets in each man's life
as a result of incremental revelations.

Those incremental disclosures provide the screenplay with its texture
and flavor. Each time the writer reveals a new facet about either
man, the story and plot take a turn into unexpected arenas. Maguire
keeps the audience guessing, and wondering if Horrigan is up to the
challenge.

---

[10] Jeff Maguire. *In the Line of Fire.* All excerpts used by permission of the author.

Horrigan and Booth play a cat and mouse game in *In the Line of Fire*. A game develops not only for the protagonist and antagonist, but for the audience as well.

We want to hear more about these characters. We want to know where they come from and what motivates the hero and the assassin. Drawn into the story by our fascination with the well-crafted characters and the relentless motion of the plot, we enter Act 3, hoping that whatever resolution the writer has prepared feels like the right one.

Action and adventure are not the only examples we can use to see the development of antagonists and protagonists.

In 1999, the film *Shakespeare in Love*, written by Marc Norman and Tom Stoppard, came on the scene. While not a contemporary story in terms of the time in which it is set, it is contemporary in tone and style.

Norman and Stoppard deliberately set out to create a screenplay that modern audiences would accept, enjoy, and appreciate for its inside jokes.

In Act 1, Viola dresses as a boy and auditions for a play. Will has never heard anyone read his lines the way this "boy," Tom, reads them. He chases "Tom" across the Thames and onto the estate of the aristocratic de Lesseps family.

Act 2 begins when Will crashes a party at the estate where the betrothal between Viola and Lord Wessex will be announced. He sees Viola, daughter of the de Lesseps who, in reality, had disguised herself as "Tom." Will is smitten on the spot as much as Romeo is smitten when he first sees Juliet at a ball.

The scene sets up the conflict between Will and Wessex, as well as the development of each personality as the story moves forward.

Wessex reacts to the presence of the poet by accosting Shakespeare at the point of a knife. Will, unarmed and astonished at this turn of events, doesn't know what he's done to deserve such treatment.

To his surprise he finds a lordly dagger at his throat.

                    WILL (continued)
                     (startled)
          How do I offend, my lord?

                    WESSEX
          By coveting my property. I cannot
          shed blood in her house but I will
          cut your throat anon. You have a
          name?

                    WILL
                    (gulps)
          Christopher Marlowe at your service.

Wessex shoves him through the nearest door.

Viola's eyes are searching the room for Will. She finds Wessex smiling at her. She looks away.[11]

Through most of the screenplay Norman and Stoppard keep Will and Wessex apart. Any contact between them comes when Will is in disguise or when Wessex believes that Shakespeare is another writer, Christopher Marlowe.

---

[11]Marc Norman & Tom Stoppard. *Shakespeare In Love*. New York : Miramax Books. 1998. p. 44 - 45.

Will's passion for Viola continues to grow just as his antipathy toward Wessex flourishes. Wessex, on the other hand, shows himself to be an increasingly boorish suitor to Viola. He makes demands. He insults her with the notion that he is only marrying her for her money.

Each escalating scene with its arch, witty, often raucous dialogue builds tension and conflict between the two men – both of whom want Viola.

Shakespeare in Love contributes a valuable lesson for all writers: It's not necessary for antagonists and protagonists to be at each other's throats literally throughout a screenplay. If the adversaries desire that which they cannot or should not have, conflict will erupt, maintaining tension in the screenplay all the way through to Act 3.

PUTTING IT ALL TOGETHER

The key to developing solid antagonists and protagonists is to give them enough strength to make them worthy opponents. Without that dynamic, stories may end up as vapid exercises in plot structure with no one to root for and no one we want to see defeated.

The backbone of any story is character. The best stories told - whether they are *Notting Hill* - like love stories or action-adventure films such as the animated *Tarzan* - have compelling characters that drive the story forward. They carry the audience with them. We want to see how they overcome adversity and defeat whatever enemies they face.

Therefore, it's necessary for writers to continually surprise the audience with how the characters grow and develop. At the same time, that growth and development must remain consistent with who these characters are.

Act 2 raises the stakes between protagonists and antagonists. Modest confrontations fought over minor problems rarely intrigue the audience. They will not sit still waiting for the third act. That showdown or climax has to prove worthwhile.

Motivation is the key to both heroes and villains. We have to ask ourselves: Is each of our characters motivated properly in order to achieve his or her goals? If that motivation appears weak, then we have to rethink how we created the characters. We have to return to the source and determine why these characters exist.

Part of Act 2's purpose is character revelation. It helps us make the antagonist and protagonist believable within the context of the genre.

Make no mistake, however, in thinking that an antagonist has to be human. It can be a machine *(Terminator)*, a tornado *(Twister)*, a meteor *(Armageddon)* or other forces of nature. On the other hand, in each of those stories a human antagonist also exists who exacerbates the situation.

Act 2 is not a way station on the road to completing the story. When it comes to developing the core of our stories, as well as our antagonists and protagonists, Act 2 becomes the central place where revelations, motivations, and confrontations take place - making the stories we create live and breathe.

EXERCISES:

View the videos of *In the Line of Fire* and *Shakespeare in Love.*

1. Describe the character revelations that help "raise the stakes" in the films.

2. Identify the story or plot point revelations that help "raise the stakes" in the films.

3. Define the differences between the character revelations that both films.

4. Define the differences between the story or plot points in both films.

Chapter Five
ENTER THE HERO

When does a hero become a hero? When does the protagonist of our story adopt the mantle of a person who takes charge and makes changes?

During Act 1, our characters prepare for the moment when they enter the conflict. They think they know what lies ahead. They believe they understand the dangers – either physical or emotional - that they may face.

At this point we have to make a major decision: Go forward and face an uncertain future, or pull back and return to the certainties of life. Since we're developing a screenplay, we have to face the conflict and resolve it, or else the story stops in its tracks at the end of Act 1.

We ought to define what heroes represent. Heroes are the protagonists of our stories. They are our leading characters and, while the word *hero* is thrown around quite often, they are not necessarily heroic figures.

They can be, and in many cases are, ordinary people thrown into unusual situations. Using their wits, wiles, and strength they have to deal with events that appear to overcome them.

Protagonists can be anyone from William Wallace, the larger-than-life heroic revolutionary leader of the Scots in *Braveheart* (1995), to Kathleen Kelly, the owner of a modest book shop in mid-town Manhattan in *You've Got Mail* (1998).

No matter who they are, each one has his or her own battle to fight. In *Braveheart* the battle is freedom from a ruthless despot.

Wallace's nemesis is none other than King Edward I of England.

In *You've Got Mail,* Kathleen Kelly battles the encroachment of a megacorporation that threatens to destroy her small, neighborhood business. Kelly's nemesis is the corporate president Joe Fox III, with whom she has fallen in love unknowingly via e-mail.

Protagonists come in many shapes, sizes, and genders. They have adventures that revolve around action, drama, love, or horror.

However, in almost all stories, Act 2 opens the way for an in-depth examination of who they are and why they act the way they do. It also gives us an opportunity to explore our protagonists' enemies and allies.

As writers who create the characters and their stories, we ought to know everything about them. Only in that way can we develop our screenplays in ways that make sense and, at the same time, surprise the audience.

The twists and turns, ambitions and desires, the needs and wants of our leading characters make these stories entertaining, satisfying tales.

Stanley Tucci, co-director, co-writer, and star of *The Big Night* (1996), and the director, co-writer, and star of *Joe Gould's Secret* (2000) based on Joseph Mitchell's book *Up in the Old Hotel,* said about characters: "...you can't live without characters, they create the plot. The imposition of a plot is not truthful. If you let the characters in a sense guide you, if you don't worry about trying to tell people and just let it happen, it will."[12]

[12] Kenneth Turan. "Directing His Trust in Pause and Effect." *Los Angeles Times.* Jan. 21, 2000. p. F1.

CHINATOWN'S LARGER-THAN-LIFE HERO

Jake Gittes, the unwitting hero of Robert Towne's *Chinatown* (1974), starts out as a small-time detective hired to locate a philandering husband. In the course of the story he grows in stature to a larger-than-life hero.

After introducing Gittes and the woman who employs him, Evelyn Mulwray, Towne moves him into the second act knowing that Evelyn's husband is an official with the water department in Los Angeles.

CHINATOWN: ACT 2 BEATS

- Gittes arrives at a reservoir as workers drag Hollis Mulwray's body out of the water. Workers suspect that he might have been inspecting a flood control channel, and was caught in a surge when water was released.

- Intrigued by the water situation in Los Angeles, Gittes has doubts about the cause of death. He suspects foul play. This draws him deeper into the story. His interest in the beautiful Evelyn Mulwray keeps him even more involved.

- He continues investigating, and runs into numerous obstacles and enemies. The fiercest are two heavies who accost him at a flood control channel and warn him to drop the case. To emphasize their point, one of them slices his nose with a knife. The action only infuriates Gittes. Now he wants the truth.

- Part of the truth emerges when he discovers that Evelyn Mulwray's father, Noah Cross, was Mulwray's partner in a crooked water scheme.

• In the middle of Act 2, Gittes accosts Cross at his own retreat. The old man attempts to hire the detective as a ruse for getting him off the story. Gittes recognizes the ploy. It only heightens Gittes desire to solve a mystery that has taken on bigger-than-life aspects.

• Another twist to the story arises when the detective finds out that the water planned for Los Angeles will be diverted to the San Fernando Valley, further enriching the remaining partner, Noah Cross.

• Gittes will not relent and heavies come down on him. However, he beats them to the punch and escapes.

• At the end of Act 2 Gittes lands in the arms of Evelyn Mulwray.

With each beat we learn something new about Jake Gittes and those surrounding him.

LEARNING ABOUT CHARACTER

In the first beat Gittes meets two members of the Los Angeles police force. The dialogue indicates they've known each other for a long time. One of them appears to hide valuable information. The other, Escobar, seems jealous of Gittes' status as a detective. This sets up a conflict that relates to the story, but also reveals part of Gittes' past.

When Gittes runs afoul of the heavies at the flood control channel in the second revelatory beat, we, through the eyes of Gittes, discover that he's on the end of a very real death threat. That points to more than a philandering husband and an accidental death. The vicious attack against him only pushes him further into the mystery.

The next major revelation for Gittes occurs when he finds out that

Noah Cross, Evelyn Mulwray's father, once owned the entire water supply for the city. Cross and Mulwray were partners. This puts a different spin on the story he was given.

Having uncovered this piece of news, Gittes confronts the formidable Noah Cross in his own lair, an elegant California rancho. Pretending to be concerned about his daughter, Cross "hires" the detective to find the girl with whom Hollis Mulwray allegedly had an affair.

This propels Gittes on an investigation in which he discovers that the water for the city will not be delivered as promised. Instead, it will go to land that has been bought up through bogus claims by Cross, Mulwray, and others. As Gittes says: "...they're conning L.A. into building it (a dam), only the water won't go to L.A. – it'll go here." Even Evelyn, Noah's daughter, has no idea of the depth of the nefarious scheme.

They arrive at a rest home for the elderly, and find the people in whose name the property has been purchased. The retirees have become unwitting dupes in a scheme to commit fraud. One landowner died a week before he purchased the land – a very odd situation.

The heavies attempt to kidnap Gittes. With Evelyn's help, he escapes. As they race away, we learn something new about Gittes. He once worked for the District Attorney. At that moment his stature rises in our eyes as well as in the eyes of the wealthy Evelyn Mulwray. He also reveals why he has a need to aid the underdog. When he worked for the DA, he tried to help someone and it backfired.

```
                    GITTES
        I thought I was keeping someone from
        being hurt and actually I ended up
```

> making sure they were hurt.

That revelatory moment expands Gittes' personality and makes him much more heroic in Evelyn's eyes. Against Gittes' better judgement the two of them make love as we enter the third act.

Throughout Act 2, Towne provides us with increasingly fascinating clues about Gittes, his life as it is and his life prior to the opening credits. Those biographical notes build a character who has dimension beyond the flat environs of the motion picture screen.

These aspects of character that Towne creates made *Chinatown* an enduring motion picture. However, the protagonist is not the complete picture. The other characters in the screenplay enrich the story's edge and classic feel.

ALLIES

The protagonist of *Chinatown* has few allies. However, the ones that exist are fully fleshed characters.

Evelyn Mulwray starts out as an almost prototypical Dashiell Hammett femme fatale – after the Mary Astor school of characterization. We're not sure what she wants or if she's a genuine person.

As the story unfolds, Towne delves deeper and deeper into her psyche. Soon we understand her feelings for Gittes. Not until the third act do we understand her need to protect her daughter.

In the second act the writer leads the audience and Gittes down other paths and into wonderful cul-de-sacs - where clues abound. However, those clues cleverly skirt the issue. They make sense only when the actual disclosure erupts in Act 3.

Just as in *The Third Man*, carefully choreographed clues foreshadow events to come. Few of the clues trumpet their announcement. If they did, the story would hold little mystery and few surprises for us.

One of the keys, therefore, to developing Act 2 and the way we present our protagonists and their allies, as well as the antagonists and their minions, is to prepare the ground so that when the unexpected occurs, the audience is not only surprised, but also understands it.

If the audience is taken unawares without having been prepared, even subliminally, the unexpected may not only come as a shock, but it will also divert attention to the lack of logic in the situation.

On the other hand, we do not want to send an e-mail message to the audience informing them specifically what our clues foreshadow. Let the story take care of that function. Permit the audience to grasp the consequences. Permit the audience to have a function in storytelling.

ENEMIES

Certainly, *Chinatown* abounds with plenty of enemies for Jake Gittes. Each of them has a unique personality that helps develop the story and hold the interest of the audience.

The main foe Gittes faces is Noah Cross, Evelyn Mulwray's crusty multimillionaire father. One of the remarkable ways Towne has of exploring Cross' personality takes place at his rancho, when Gittes interviews him.

```
EXT. BRIDLE PATH — GITTES & CROSS

walking toward the main house — a classic
Monterey.  A horse led on a halter by another
```

ranch hand slows down and defecates in the center of the path they are taking. Gittes doesn't
notice.

>   CROSS
>   Horseshit.

Gittes pauses, not certain he has heard correct-
ly.

>   GITTES
>   Sir?

>   CROSS
>   I said horseshit.
>   (pointing)
>   Horseshit.

>   GITTES
>   Yes, sir, that's what it looks
>   like — I'll give you that.

Cross pauses when they reach the dung pile. He
removes his hat and waves it, inhales deeply.

>   CROSS
>   Love the smell of it. A lot of
>   people do but of course they
>   won't admit it. Look at the
>   shape.

Gittes glances down out of politeness.

>   CROSS
>   (continuing; smiling,
>   almost enthusiastic)
>   Always the same.

Cross walks on. Gittes follows.

                    GITTES
              (not one to let it
              go)
          Always?

                    CROSS
          What? Oh, damn near — yes.
          Unless the animal's sick or
          something.
                (stops and glances
                back)
          and the steam rising off it
          like that in the morning — that's
          life, Mr. Gittes. Life.

They move on.

                    CROSS
              (continuing)
          Perhaps this preoccupation with
          horseshit may seem a little
          perverse, but I ask you to
          remember this — one way or
          another, it's what I've dealt
          in all my life. Let's have
          breakfast.[13]

That wonderful vignette explains almost everything we need to know
about Cross. It's also a warning to Gittes that this is a man who will
stop at nothing to get his way. He's walked in the dirt and is willing
to continue doing it for the rest of his life, and no one had better get
in his way.

---

[13] Robert Towne. *Chinatown*. All excerpts by permission of the author.

Towne writes the scene almost as if it were comic relief. Only later do we realize that we've been set up to accept Cross' incestuous behavior, and we're shocked to find the truth. However, by clever foreshadowing in the second act, the writer prepares us for the impact of the revelation unconsciously.

JUMPING THE HURDLES

Each step along the way reveals more and more about the protagonist and his antagonists. They also reveal information about his allies and supposed allies.

No one in *Chinatown* is all good or all bad. The characters have dimensions all their own, and Towne explores the how and why of their motivations. He weaves the revelations into the fabric of the story – in this case the second act.

Exposition is used sparingly, and only as it works within the confines of the story and its characters. Towne does not engage in polemics or messages. The information he wishes to impart to the audience comes in bits and pieces.

The lesson for all writers is that it's not necessary to slam the audience in the face with information. It can be done subtly and with finesse, giving the story a fine and satisfying edginess.

PUTTING IT ALL TOGETHER

The second act permits our protagonists to enter the arena where conflict takes place. Here is where they can explore all the options we present to them.

Once the door opens, our creativity kicks in by delving into the "who" and "why" of characters. In order to do that, we have to know their needs and wants. The only way to understand those elements is to have intimate knowledge of our characters.

Revealing these to the audience is the next step in Act 2. That is best done subtly and carefully, so that the clues provided do not appear obvious. They ought to give the audience enough information without tipping off the surprises we have in store for them.

Exposition explaining various aspects of characters should weave itself throughout the fabric of the story we wish to tell. In that way, we hold the audience's interest and help our characters propel the story toward its climax and resolution.

EXERCISES:

1. Write a brief biography of your main character, taking him or her up to the beginning of your story. The biography should include the following:

> **A.** Family of origin
> **B.** Siblings (if any)
> **C.** Relationship with parents and siblings
> **D.** Education
> **E.** Trauma in your character's life
> **F.** Relationships with peers and significant others
> **G.** Weaknesses and strengths (abilities, talent, intelligence, etc.)

2. Describe the protagonist you created.

> **A.** Larger than life? How have you presented that information?
> **B.** Reality-based? How have you shown that information?

Chapter Six
THE BIG BATTLE

In order to create interesting stories, something extraordinary must happen during the course of the screenplay. Great screenplays have fascinating characters who grab the story and drive it to its ultimate conclusion. On that drive, our protagonists have to fight, brawl and crawl their way over and through all kinds of barriers.

Those impediments may turn out to be real. For example, an innocent, gentle man battles an implacable enemy whose only desire is to destroy a people and render a nation free of a particular ethnic group - as in *Life is Beautiful* (1998).

Obstacles may be figurative. Internal demons rise up and torment the troubled protagonist of *The Apostle* (1997), who wrestles with his own sins in order to save his soul.

Whatever the leading characters in our stories want or need, they should not achieve it easily. The second act gives us room and opportunity to build bumps in the road over which they ride; to erect barricades over which they have to climb; to launch attacks against which they must defend themselves.

Rising tension and conflict are the hallmarks of Act 2. Therefore, how those obstacles are presented becomes important to the story and the way it develops.

Take another look at the graph of the second act of *The Third Man* on page 64. Each beat becomes a heightened revelation, a moment of danger, a hurdle that must be leaped leading to more exciting moments. Those beats draw the audience further into the story.

As Jake Gittes moves through *Chinatown*, he discovers more and more mystery and confusion surrounding murder, greed, lust, and incest. The audience wants to know what will happen next.

The Third Man and *Chinatown* portray their protagonists as outsiders. The audience finds itself in these characters' shoes working their way through the story from the characters' points of view.

DISCOVERY OF TRUTH

Truth in a screenplay becomes whatever we wish it to be. Our characters reach toward it once they cross into the second act. Unraveling the mystery or solving the puzzle that surrounds them ought to be our main goal.

We drop our main characters into mysterious, uncertain, confusing, enigmatic situations. We create them with certain abilities and talents, and present them with choices. Now we expect them to swim out in a lake of unknown depth in order to reach the opposite shore, and find some kind of definitive resolution awaiting them.

Eventually, truth is revealed. However, the second act need not permit our protagonists to know they have found the truth until the burgeoning resolution that comes in the third act - or at least not until after it appears that our main characters have in some way been defeated. Defeat, however, has a variety of meanings in the context of a story or screenplay. It can be physical or psychological, depending on the genre of the tale.

TRUTH AS SHOCK

Three Days of the Condor has a turning point in the second act that propels the main character, Turner, toward the climax.

He escapes from the heavies who assassinated his co-workers at a CIA front organization. Turner kidnaps a woman, Katherine Hale, and forces her to take him to her apartment so he can hide out.

Katherine agrees to assist him. Meanwhile, Turner tries to determine who the culprits are. As he recalls the events of the previous morning he remembers his chief informing him that someone in the CIA at Langley, Virginia, had dismissed his interpretation of a supposed code. The name of the Washington Section Chief is Wicks.

At that moment, the doorbell rings and a man masquerading as a mail carrier attempts to murder Turner. Turner eventually kills him. On the man's body he discovers a note with a phone number and an extension.

He calls the number in New York, but there's no such extension. Then he calls the same number at a Washington, D.C. area code.

Turner on the telephone.

> VOICE ON PHONE
> Six-three-one-one.

> TURNER
> CIA?   Langley?

> VOICE ON PHONE
> Six-three-one-one.

> TURNER
> Extension one-eight-nine-one.

> VOICE
> Extension one-eight-nine-one.

                          TURNER
              Let me speak to Mr. Wicks.

                          VOICE
              He's not here just now. May I
              ask who's calling, please?

Turner quickly hangs up the telephone.

INT. KATHERINE'S CAR — DAY

As they drive toward Washington.

                        KATHERINE
              What did you do to those people?

                          TURNER
              What people? I don't know who they
              are. I file a report and a guy in
              Washington reads it — is supposed to
              read it. He's my Section Chief. He
              comes to New York to kill me.[14]

Once he discovers the reality of his situation, he begins to take control, even though it seems as if one man alone cannot possibly defeat a powerful enemy with seemingly unlimited resources.

Turner sets the wheels in motion, turning the tide against his antagonists. Believing that the assassin will come after him, Turner keeps up his guard.

Multiple twists and turns pile one on top of another throughout Act 2. Writers Semple and Rayfield have the insight to understand that whatever Turner accomplishes always falls well within his expertise.

---

[14] Lorenzo Semple, Jr. *Three Days of the Condor*. All excerpts by permission of the author.

The first act foreshadows much of what we know about his independence and iconoclastic nature. He is an expert cryptographer, therefore able to pull bits and pieces of information together to create meaning. Turner is adept at repairing mechanical devices. He is physically fit, demonstrated by the fact that he rides a bicycle to work every morning – albeit a motorized bike.

Surprises blossom in the screenplay. A rogue group operates within the CIA. Turner has unwittingly discovered why it came into being. It has something to do with oil in the Middle East.

Soon we learn that not everyone in the Agency is bad, and that they have been on the lookout for rogues. They see Turner as an impediment to their investigation. He finds himself between the proverbial rock and a hard place.

He plans to reveal what he knows to the public through the media, believing that this will lessen the danger to his life as well as breathe fresh air into the secretive government agency.

All of this works well in the thriller genre. Escalating action and danger keep the audience rooting for the hero as he avenges himself on the villains.

Three Days of the Condor shows how important it is for writers to understand all their characters' faults and strong points, and how to use them within the boundaries of the universe they create.

In the action-thriller, conflict should be built firmly on the story's premise so that when protagonists face ever-escalating moments of tension, how they overcome them makes sense. We have to lay the groundwork by indicating their intelligence, cunning, mental and physical strengths, and limitations. *Three Days of the Condor* offers revelations that open doors for the heroes and permits them to carry out a plan of action that leads to a thrilling resolution.

If we examine carefully the screenplays of *The Third Man, Three Days of the Condor*, or *Chinatown*, we discover that the writers keep upping the ante for the main characters. Every time protagonists find themselves escaping from a dangerous situation, they immediately discover that they've fallen into a deeper hole.

How they extricate themselves from danger depends upon the nature of the characters. Some will use their intelligence. Others may utilize brute strength. Whatever way they overcome adversity ought to remain consistent the personalities, traits, and motivations writers create for them.

THE HIDDEN TRUTH

Truth that isn't apparent to the characters can also occur in the second act. Those scenes may seem to glide by the protagonists, although the audience recognizes them.

When Harry Met Sally... (1989), a romantic comedy written by Nora Ephron, is filled with such events.

The story revolves around two single people, Harry and Sally, who meet after Sally has come out of a disastrous relationship and Harry wants to get out of his commitment.

Harry and Sally develop a wonderful friendship that blossoms into love neither one of them will admit to, because they wish to remain friends. It's their belief that once they make a commitment to each other their friendship will end.

The moment of truth arrives at a New Year's Eve party. Harry and Sally have no dates, but they have each other. All around them they see couples together. Acting as friends, they dance and talk around the issue of their relationship. During the scene a moment occurs when the spark between them becomes brighter: "...we see the beginning of something...an inkling...a little tender moment."[15] It ends abruptly when the countdown to the New Year starts.

They step out on a balcony. Feeling slightly uncomfortable, they see all the other couples hugging and kissing. Harry and Sally wish each other a happy new year and kiss. The kiss is perfunctory and awkward. The sense that Ephron gives the audience is that they want it to be more than friendly, but after all they've said and been through, they now find it difficult to express their true feelings.

Ephron builds the scene by letting us know that Harry and Sally care deeply for each other. On the other hand, the setup throughout the second act reveals two people who continually skirt the issue of how they feel about one another.

In the introduction to the printed version of the screenplay, Nora Ephron explores the subtext of the comedy: "The truth is that men don't want to be friends with women. Men don't understand women and they don't much care... Women on the other hand, are dying to be friends with men. Women know they don't understand men, and it bothers them: they think that if only they could be friends with them, they would understand them."[16]

The relationship between Harry and Sally receives a jump-start in a scene that follows shortly. Here the characters still don't understand the depth of their feelings for one another and why they fit together.

Harry agrees to set up his friend Jess with Sally. Sally sets up her friend Marie with Harry. The four meet in a restaurant and it becomes apparent that Jess and Marie are actually the ones attracted to each other.

[15] Nora Ephron. *When Harry Met Sally...* New York: Alfred A. Knopf. 1990. p. 53.

[16] Ibid. p. xvi.

As they walk along Broadway, the scene takes a not unexpected turn.

It turns out that Jess likes Marie more than he likes Sally, Marie likes Jess more than she likes Harry. The scene plays between the two women and the two men who walk together. Sally warns Marie not to hurt Harry's feelings since "...he's going through a rough period, and I just don't want you to reject him right now." At the same time, Harry warns Jess not to hurt Sally's feelings because "...Sally's very vulnerable right now." [17]

The scene ends when Jess and Marie dive into a cab, leaving Harry and Sally alone on the street. Ephron cranks up the emotional engine for the protagonists. The scene informs everyone, except Harry and Sally, about the true nature of their relationship. They belong together. The harder they try to remain platonic friends, the more apparent it becomes to everyone, except the two people involved, that they love each other.

Throughout the second act, Ephron presents us with scene after scene involving dates, chance encounters, and a budding romance that blossoms. The main characters can't see it, and the flower hangs on the vine unnoticed. In this way, Act 2 opens the story to discoveries that push the characters forward.

When Harry Met Sally... has revelations that the characters either refuse to see or understand until the final moments of the story. That's what makes the humor in the screenplay work. The audience is in on the joke. The audience feels the comic angst of the characters and becomes part of the secret.

PUTTING IT ALL TOGETHER

One of the key aspects of Act 2 is the evolution of the crisis or series of crises for our protagonists. These developments support our

[17]Ibid. p. 60.

characters in their quest to solve their problems.

However, crises alone cannot maintain the forward motion of the story. They represent moments leading toward a revelation, or series of revelations, that have to do with dire physical dangers or emotional dilemmas in the lives of our characters.

Successful screenplays usually have twists and turns in the plot of the story that build on one another throughout the second act. Protagonists climb over those obstacles in order to reach the climax of the story and resolve the adventure, the love story, the science-fiction epic, or whatever the genre of the motion picture may be.

By encountering these barricades and clambering over them, our characters can then begin to unravel the mystery. They have to ask themselves: "Why is that obstacle in my way and who put it there?"

Before reaching that point, the conflict usually leads to some kind of truth. That truth represents what we, the creators of the story, wish it to represent.

The major moment of truth occurs when our characters discover their physical or emotional dangers - and what or who has created them.

Windows begin to open at the center point of Act 2 permitting light to shine into the dark corners of the story. Our characters use those glimmerings to gather their resources, in order to spin off into the last half of the second act. The discovery of what appears to be the truth places our protagonists on the road that leads them to their big reward.

EXERCISES:

1. Describe the "truth" your main character discovers in your own screenplay.

2. Plot in outline form the crisis or series of crises that occur in Act 2 of your screenplay.

    A. Identify how the crises build on the first act's setup.
    B. Describe how they advance the story toward the third act.
    C. Indicate how they support your character's ability to solve his or her problem(s).

Chapter Seven
RUN FOR THE MONEY

While discovering the truth is a major revelation that takes place in Act 2, it becomes only a step toward the protagonists' recovery of the reward or attainment of the seemingly unattainable.

Depending on the genre of story, that reward can appear in the shape of money, love, friendship, or new information that confirms our heroes' suspicions. The search for the elusive prize becomes the centerpiece of the last half of the second act.

Act 2 should also accomplish another task: developing the viewer's emotional investment in the main character. Without this development, the screenplay will come off as a series of dull incidents, occurring to characters in which the audience has little interest. The audience ought to care for the characters. They do not have to love them, but they should have an abiding interest in them, strong enough to want to continue following them through the rest of the story.

In order to understand how the search operates, it's necessary to look at a variety of genres to see how other writers handle obtaining the reward.

THE INTANGIBLE REWARD

In the Oscar-winning Italian film of 1998, *Life is Beautiful (La Vita è Bella)*, written by Roberto Benigni and Vincenzo Cerami, the Nazis round up the hero, Guido; his son, Joshua; and his wife, Dora; and ship them to a concentration camp somewhere in Italy.

Almost everyone realizes they are in mortal danger. People are routinely murdered. To protect his son, Guido pretends that it's all a game – a strange game, but a game nevertheless.

Guido has to convince his son that the filthy, squalid surroundings in which they find themselves are part of the game. That opportunity arises when German soldiers rattle off a stern warning about the behavior of the internees.

Joshua listens in awed astonishment as Guido volunteers to translate from German to Italian. In reality, Guido does not understand a word of German. His goal is to make the game real for his son. If he can accomplish this task, he will have attained the one reward he most desires: saving Joshua from the horror of their situation.

```
...an SS CORPORAL comes in with two armed sol-
diers.  The corporal is a pudgy man with a stern
air about him.  He looks over his shoulder as
though waiting for someone.  But he's in a
hurry.
                    CORPORAL
                 (in German)
         Any of you Italians speak German?

No one says a word, they are too frightened.
Guido says in a whisper to Bartholomew,

                    GUIDO
                 (whispering)
         What did he say?


                    BARTHOLOMEW
                 (very softly)
         He's looking for someone who speaks
         German.  He's going to explain the
         camp rules.
```

Guido promptly raises his hand.

> BARTHOLOMEW
> (very softly)
> You speak German?

The corporal motions Guido to come stand next to him.

> GUIDO
> (very softly as he moves)
> No.

Guido takes his place next to the corporal, who immediately starts yelling loudly at the prisoners.

> CORPORAL
> (in German)
> Attention! I'm only going to say this once!

He looks at Guido, waiting for a translation.

> GUIDO
> Okay, the game begins! If you're here, you're here, if you're not, you're not.

> CORPORAL
> (in German)
> You are here for one reason, and one reason only!

> GUIDO
> (in Italian)
> The first one to get a thousand
> points wins a real tank!

> CORPORAL
> (in German)
> To work!

> GUIDO
> Lucky man!

The prisoners are trying to understand what the
corporal and Guido are talking about, but only
Joshua gets it. He is standing very still, eyes
popping.

The corporal points to the yard outside.

> CORPORAL
> Any sabotage is punishable by death,
> sentence carried out right here in
> the yard, by machine gun in the back!

He points to his own back.

> GUIDO
> Scores will be announced every morn-
> ing on the loudspeakers outside!
> Whoever is last has to wear a sign
> that says "jackass" — here on his
> back!

Imitating the corporal's gesture, he points to
his own back.[18]

---

[18] Roberto Benigni & Vincenzo Cerami. *Life is Beautiful*. Used by permission of Jean Vigo Italia.

Once Guido establishes his own rules and convinces his son that this is all a contest, he must carry it out to its end.

The other prisoners play along with him in their own desire to protect the young boy. As a result of the "game," the dread heightens and the humor becomes more farcical.

The audience grasps Guido's character from the very beginning of the screenplay, where Benigni and Cerami establish him as an iconoclastic, childlike innocent with an incredibly rich imagination.

For him to embark on this preposterous scheme makes sense because of who he is, what we have seen him do, and his motivation: he loves his wife and adores his son. He will do anything he can to protect them from the harsh realities of a world turned upside-down by war and racial hatred. The writers underscore Guido's incredible sense of humor as well as his humanity.

The reward in *Life is Beautiful* is not a tangible object. It consists of making life as wonderful as possible in a time and place where it seems almost incomprehensible to imagine anything beautiful.

Benigni and Cerami achieve a fairy tale moment, making the dread of the camp even more palpable by using a collision of opposites: the harsh orders of the Nazis mirrored against Guido's outrageously playful "translation."

They also foreshadow Guido's fate when the Corporal announces what will happen to prisoners suspected of sabotage. When that scene occurs in Act 3 we are shocked and saddened, but not surprised.

Foreshadowing plays a major part in *Life is Beautiful*. Clues that seem benign reveal themselves as action in the second half of the second act. Benigni and Cerami understand the necessity of planting clues, and then permitting the audience to forget them until the time comes for them to surface once more in a clearer light.

Roberto Benigni explains the process: "...you put the seeds in the first part, and the flowers in the second part come back... You have to laugh in the moment, and you forget. Then when it comes back, this is very good."[19]

THE TANGIBLE REWARD

It's much easier to deal with stories where rewards can be manipulated, touched, even cashed in. However, real rewards can also come from taking what appears as the truth and ripping off the outer layers to reveal what's happening underneath.

Sometimes those rewards are the confirmation of long-held suspicions. Or they can be achieved when our protagonists come to terms with their inner demons and doubts.

Jeff Maguire's screenplay *In the Line of Fire* (1993) explores two major themes: the real reward of capturing an assassin, and the intangible reward of self-redemption.

Chapter 4 describes the simple story line of the film. It's the second, or B, story line - examining Horrigan's own demons - that makes the screenplay fascinating. When the assassination plot in *In the Line of Fire* starts to evolve, Horrigan sees it as a way to rid himself of his guilt.

The critical beats in Act 2 demonstrate how Maguire builds the conflict between protagonist and antagonist, and develops the emotional push and pull that invests the audience in Horrigan's story.

---

[19]Susan Billington Katz. "A Conversation with Roberto Benigno." *Written By:* Dec./Jan. 1999. Vol. 3, Issue 1, p. 65.

- Horrigan passes out while running alongside the President's limousine, setting up the premise that perhaps he's past his prime as an agent.

- Booth phones Horrigan and taunts him about his drinking. Could Horrigan have miscalculated, keeping him from saving John F. Kennedy's life?

- Horrigan finds himself attracted to Lilly, a female agent. He wonders if she finds him attractive, thus proving he's still a "man."

- Horrigan spots Booth in a crowd in Washington. He loses the man, but retrieves Booth's fingerprints.

- He is surprised when the FBI can find no files on the prints. This leads to suspicion as to Booth's true identity.

- Horrigan's iconoclastic attitude almost leads to his dismissal from the presidential security force.

- The President makes a speech and a balloon pops. Horrigan overreacts and his chief takes him to task for embarrassing the President.

- Booth taunts Horrigan over the telephone about the balloon incident. Apparently he was in the audience.

- Horrigan discovers that Booth (who is actually named Leary) was a CIA operative.

- Horrigan closes in on Leary, only to discover that the killer has no fear of dying. He expects to die in a hail of gunfire after he takes out the President.

Revelations about the protagonist come mainly from the antagonist, who triggers Horrigan into a dark and anxiety-ridden self-examination.

Revelations concerning the antagonist derive from clues the agent puts together like a jigsaw puzzle, except for those moments when we see Booth in action. The writer creates scenes that highlight the vicious cold-blooded assassin, making him an even worthier opponent for our hero.

About twenty minutes into Act 2, Booth telephones Horrigan at Secret Service headquarters. He reveals what he knows about the agent, including the fact that Horrigan had pleaded with Kennedy to use the bulletproof bubbletop limousine.

Later Booth reveals information about Horrigan's personal life. All of it is designed to set up a smoke screen and convince the agent that he is not capable of acting against Booth.

Horrigan begins to put together a profile of his antagonist - suspecting that Booth's motives are deeper than just a psychotic nightmare. Trained as a killer, Booth has no other means of venting his frustrations. Having been dismissed from the Agency, Booth has decided to make one last stand.

He admits his strange reasoning to Horrigan during one of his many taunting phone calls:

```
                    BOOTH
                  (laughs)
        You're the same as me, Frank… I've
        seen where you choose to live…
        I've watched you alone in your bar…
```

```
          All we've got left is the game…
          That's why fate brought us together
          You're on the defense — I'm on
          offense.
```

The cat and mouse game continues as the screenwriter, Jeff Maguire, cranks the excitement level higher and higher. The clock continues to tick toward the moment when the President will make his appearance. Horrigan believes he's getting closer and closer to Booth. Inevitably, the man eludes him.

When Booth calls again near the end of the second act, Horrigan is ready. He tells Booth he knows his identity. If Booth turns himself in, he can make a deal.

The big surprise for Horrigan and the audience comes when Booth admits that he wants to die. Therefore, nothing anyone can say will stop him. This places the agent in the position of going after someone who has no reason to give up.

Maguire sets it all up in a few brief speeches:

```
                    BOOTH
          I let them transform me into what
          they wanted me to be… I can't
          even remember who I was before
          they sunk their claws into me.
          Then one day, I'm of no further use
          to them.  So they decide to terminate
          me.  Did they tell you that, Frank?
          Did they tell you they sent a friend
          of mine to kill me?
```

```
Frank looks over at Sam.
```

> BOOTH
> I have a terminal illness, Frank.
> I know too much to be allowed to
> live. And that's a big problem for
> you, because most people who are
> smart enough to kill the President
> are also smart enough to know they
> can't get away with it, but you see,
> I don't care… One way or another, I'm
> a dead man.

> FRANK
> Let me bring you in, Leary… Let
> me see what I can work out.

> BOOTH
> I appreciate your concern, Frank.
> But it's too late. We can't call the
> game now. I plan to die on my terms.
> Not yours, or theirs.

On one level, Horrigan must prevent the assassination from taking place because that's his job. On another level, he needs to defeat Leary in order to cleanse himself of his perceived guilt regarding Kennedy.

Act 2 of the screenplay cleverly sets up Horrigan's guilt and bulldog-like resolve played against Leary's intense determination. Maguire creates a character who has a difficult time permitting anyone to know the anger within. Even when Horrigan meets a caring woman, he has difficulty letting her in.

Through Leary we learn that Horrigan is divorced and has a young daughter he rarely visits. Since we stand in Horrigan's shoes throughout the story, the writer achieves the effect of keeping us at a distance from his personal life. We never meet his ex-wife or his child.

Act 2 of *In the Line of Fire* takes us through twists and turns in the plot, but also the twists and turns of the main character's life. Although the clock ticking on the coming assassination maintains tension in the screenplay, it's the personal story that holds our interest. The audience wants to know how Horrigan will handle this pressure-filled situation, while Leary continues taunting him about his life and his apparent failures.

FOCUS ON THE CHARACTERS

In both *Life is Beautiful* and *In the Line of Fire*, the writers maintain focus on their protagonists: Guido and Horrigan. We become invested in their lives, their dreams, and their fortunes. Because we care about who they are, all through the second act we want them to win the reward they seek.

They have learned the truth and now they must grab the prize. The prize can be self-redemption, beating the odds, protecting loved ones, or defeating a very real enemy.

PUTTING IT ALL TOGETHER

Rewards that our main characters seek come in many forms. They can be as real as gold discovered in hidden chests or they can be the reward of discovering the self.

No single aspect of a screenplay stands alone. We have to use each moment to reveal something new about plot and character, or else the story may become as motionless and murky as a pool of stagnant water.

113

The rewards our protagonists reach for may be actual or ephemeral. If they are tangible, we should make them worthy of our hero. If they're intangible, they ought to represent overarching moral or emotional victories so that audiences feel satisfied by the result.

Very often there's an element of both in obtaining the reward. *Life is Beautiful* not only has the intangible reward of a father protecting his child from the horrors of reality by creating a fantasy world, but also has the reward of overcoming and confusing a real enemy.

In the Line of Fire has the principal goal of preventing a murder from taking place and capturing a would-be assassin. At the same time, another reward for the main character involves overcoming internal demons.

These two examples demonstrate how protagonists achieve their rewards based on who they are, their motivations, and the changes that take place as they move through the story.

Achieving the reward offers us the opportunity to reveal more about our characters without the need for lengthy expository scenes. As we enter this part of the screenplay, we can disclose information in discreet bits of dialogue and action that infiltrate the body of knowledge we present to the audience about our characters and their lives.

EXERCISES:

1. View the video of *Life is Beautiful.* Describe the "seeds" in Act 1 and characterize how they "flower" in Act 2. (See Benigni quote on page 108.)

2. Review your own screenplay and state how you created foreshadowing in Act 1 that pays off in Act 2.

3. What "reward" does your main character wish to achieve?

    A. Tangible: Describe what it is and how it will be granted.
    B. Intangible: Explain how you created the notion in the reader/audience's mind.
    C. Tangible and Intangible: Identify the differences and how they converge.

Chapter Eight
THE BIG RACE

In previous chapters we explored how some of the finest writers establish their characters – both heroes and villains. We examined how they bolster excitement during the second act by ratcheting up the audience's expectations and the characters' drives to search for their treasures and seek truths.

Near the end of Act 2 the creative fires turn up even higher. All the story complications will not mean a thing unless we propel our characters and the audience into the third act.

Once our protagonists have found their "truth" and grabbed the reward, they usually find themselves pursued by those who want it back. Motion pictures have always used this technique expertly. But it's not only in films that we see the chase and its consequences. We find it in legends, myths, and fairy tales.

In the Greek myth *The Golden Fleece*, Jason promises to marry the sorceress Medea if she will help him steal the fleece that belongs to her father, the king. She helps Jason retrieve the fleece, and he marries her.

The king pursues Jason, his men, and Medea. They escape. Then Jason learns the lesson of many myths: "Be careful what you wish for. You may get it." Medea turns her sorcery on him.

Fairy tales present a different version of the pursuit. In the Grimm's fairy tale *The Raven*, a queen becomes irritated at her daughter, and wishes the girl would turn into a raven and fly away. Of course, that's exactly what happens. When the princess (as the raven) meets a stranger, she informs him that he can set her free if he follows certain rules.

The man promises, but fails and falls asleep. The princess leaves behind a gold ring. The stranger wakes, and in his anxiousness to set the princess free, pursues her through a series of adventures until he finds her atop a glass mountain. He rescues her and they end up getting married and - as in almost every fairy tale - live happily ever after.

The two morals of the story are that one must keep promises, and that anything of value is worth pursuing.

Both stories have been replicated time and again by motion pictures - from Charlie Chaplin's *The Immigrant* (1917) to *Enemy of the State* (1998) written by David Marconi, to *Notting Hill* (1999), written by Richard Curtis.

THE REAL PURSUIT

Pursuit is a staple of story-telling. Writers build one gut-wrenching event on top of another in order to keep adrenaline rushing through the veins of the audience.

Enemy of the State, for example, plays on the paranoia that many of us feel about the intrusion into our private lives - by the government and corporations - through the proliferation of electronic devices. The screenplay focuses on an innocent man dragged into a danger-ous situation.

Robert Dean, a high-profile attorney who takes on pro bono cases, inadvertently comes in contact with an old friend who has a video recording implicating an official of the National Security Agency with the murder of a well known congressman.

As a result, Dean's life is electronically destroyed. He discovers his credit cards cancelled, his phones tapped, etc. Phony news stories emerge, creating a schism in his marriage.

The heavies pursue the attorney with the goal of retrieving the recording. Brill, a private undercover agent who worked for Dean on occasion, reveals why Dean's pursuers won't identify themselves and tell him what they want.

                    BRILL
        They're spooks, they hate exposure.
        They wanna learn what you know, then
        deal with it. In the meantime,
        they've fucked you electronically,
        assassinated your character. You're
        nothing now.
           (Dean can't believe it)
        Now you know. You gave me some work
        over the last year. We'll call it
        even. Avoid the traps. Phones, Nets,
        mail of any kind. Anything electronic
        you do'll clue 'em in to you.
        Remember that, you may survive.
        Adios.[20]

The pursuit near the end of Act 2 has a startling beginning. Dean discovers the murder of a young woman with whom he had once been intimate. He becomes implicated in the crime, although he convinces his wife that he's innocent.

The writer uses intense, informative dialogue to reveal their motivations.

                    DEAN
        They're trying to frame me. Zavitz
        had something they wanted. Whatever
        it was, they think he gave it to

[20] David Marconi. "Enemy of the State." *Scenario: The Magazine of Screenwriting Art.* Spring 1999. Vol. 5, No. 1, p. 94.

> me before he died. They're doing
> anything they can to get to me,
> including setting me up for a murder
> I didn't commit.[21]

The chase at the end of Act 2 takes Dean to his son's school, where he retrieves a video game hidden in a Christmas gift package by his acquaintance, Zavitz, in Act 1. It has the damaging video recording encoded on it. He escapes from the heavies once more, and we move into Act 3, where Brill re-enters the story.

By examining the relentless beats of the chase that begin in the middle of Act 2, we can visualize how revelations occur, and the method by which the writer hurls the audience into the third act.

- Dean meets the real Brill who warns him that nothing he does is secret. Dean becomes trapped in a hotel room. He starts a fire that brings the police and firefighters. Injured, he's transported away from the heavies by ambulance.

- He jumps from the ambulance and the heavies pursue him into a traffic tunnel. He escapes through a ventilation shaft.

- Dean goes to his wife and convinces her he's innocent. Once again the heavies are on his tail and she helps him escape.

- He waits for his son at school and finds the evidence he needs.

- Dean goes to Rachel's (his ex-girlfriend) apartment and discovers her murdered, with clues left behind that incriminate him in her death.

- He asks Brill for help who agrees after discovering that Rachel has been murdered.

---

[21] Ibid. p. 97.

- The heavies locate Brill's hideout and it appears that the game is up by the end of Act 2.

David Marconi does a dynamic job of writing a thriller-chase by feeding on our distrust of big government and multinational corporations. He also conveys the sense that one person, if dedicated enough, can make a difference.

Enemy of the State represents the thriller-chase that doesn't stop. Unmerciful in its onslaught on the senses, it keeps up nonstop pressure. With all of its high-stakes action and melodramatic punch, *Enemy of the State* still depicts a fairy tale-like story in which the prince, after undertaking numerous dangerous tasks, defeats the dragon in its own lair and comes out with the prize.

PURSUIT AS METAPHOR

If there is any doubt that some writers know exactly what they are doing when they write their screenplays, Richard Curtis, who wrote *Notting Hill*, states: "The film is a concealed fairy tale - the Princess and the Woodcutter as it were – but we tried to make it seem as though this sort of thing might actually happen..."[22]

Almost every story has a challenge. Usually protagonists hold something precious. Even if the object of the chase is love, someone else or something else will want to steal it away. Therefore, protagonists become targets.

Three objects of pursuit exist in *Notting Hill*. One is the seemingly unattainable, glamorous motion picture actress, Anna Scott. The second is William Thacker, the charming, self-effacing owner of a small bookstore. The third is the pursuit of love.

---

[22] Richard Curtis. *Notting Hill*. London: Hodder & Stoughton. 1999.

The story combines aspects of Propp's fairy tale themes along with Todorov's theory of opposites: the pursuit of emotions, the possibility of lost love, and the need to overcome the incredible odds of the love between a commoner (bookstore owner) and royalty (the movie star.)

In the second half of Act 2, William believes that he has a special relationship with Anna - only to discover that her famous actor boyfriend has moved in with her. This presents the hero with a major obstacle.

Time passes, in which William tries to overcome his perceived loss. Anna reappears during a period in her life when she needs a friend. She admits he has been on her mind and that the incident with the boyfriend was brief and a mistake.

That night they make love and all their problems seem resolved. In the morning, however, they discover press hordes massed at William's front door. All of a sudden, the scandal she tried to escape comes home.

Anna views the moment as the ultimate betrayal:

> ANNA
> This is such a mess. I come to you
> to protect myself against more crappy
> gossip and now I'm landed in it all
> over again. For God's sake, I've got
> a boyfriend.

> WILLIAM
> You do?

It's a difficult moment — defining where they stand.

ANNA
As far as they're concerned I do.
And now tomorrow there'll be pictures
of you in every newspaper from here
to Timbuktu.

WILLIAM
I know, I know — but... just — let's
stay calm...

ANNA
You can stay calm — it's the perfect
situation for you — minimum input,
maximum publicity. Everyone you ever
bump into will know. 'Well done you
— you slept with that actress — we've
seen the pictures.'

WILLIAM
That's spectacularly unfair.

ANNA
Who knows, it may even help business.
Buy a boring book about Egypt from
the guy who screwed Anna Scott.[23]

The scene becomes the defining incident near the end of Act 2. It
provides the audience with an incentive to want to know what happens next. The scene gives the audience empathy with a hero who
did nothing wrong but has responsibility thrust upon him. It also
provides Anna with an understandable edge, and a sense of danger
to her reputation. Most of all, it presents the audience with the
notion of love lost and the hope that some kind of redemption may
come about in Act 3.

---

[23] Richard Curtis. *Notting Hill.* Used by permission of the author.

The chase in *Notting Hill* is figurative because the characters pursue love and happiness. In Act 2 Anna and William appear to lose them and then regain them - only to lose them once more.

This gives the writer an opportunity to create a modern fairy tale in which the characters may eventually live happily ever after. It also furnishes the screenwriter with a jumping off place to enter Act 3 and develop a satisfying resolution to the story.

PUTTING IT ALL TOGETHER

The chase, the pursuit, or the quest in the second act should lead our protagonists to discover some kind of truth or special knowledge.

The antagonists need to prevent that truth or knowledge from being revealed – if it's a real threat. On the other hand, emotional truth or knowledge can frighten both protagonists and antagonists.

Modeled very often on myths and legends, screenplays usually turn to fairy tale-like formulas for their execution. Protagonists are expected to win either the treasure or the one they love. The pursuit for either one may appear dangerous and filled with all sorts of pit-falls, but eventually our heroes win the day.

The Act 2 pursuit may lead characters to dead ends or seemingly impossible situations, from which they have to escape using their wits and/or strength.

Metaphorical quests, on the other hand, may involve emotional loss and gain. They may embrace the pursuit of an ideal discovered; the chase after a love once found, then lost; or the search for a promise to come.

The notion of the big race need not be limited to obvious elements in a screenplay. Almost every story uses the pursuit of something of value as its basis. Act 3 would be almost impossible without the anxiety from the characters infiltrating the audience.

EXERCISES:

Almost all stories involve either literal or figurative pursuits.

1. Identify whether your main character is the pursuer or the pursued.

2. Explain what your character is running after. Describe what your character flees from.

3. Indicate the metaphors you used to express the chase, the pursuit, and your character's quest.

Chapter Nine
THE BIG FINISH

The setup in Act 1 and the conflict of Act 2 foreshadow things to come. In previous chapters we examined elements that eventually find their way into the body of the story. Those clues help audiences understand the writer's logic. The conclusion of a screenplay ought to have a satisfying edge that digs into emotions, erupts with passion, frightens with diabolical evil, or gives us a unique touch of humor. Such a resolution of the story arrives in the third act. However, without the conflict in Act 2, it may come off as contrived at best, or illogical at its worst.

If for some reason we present moments that seem to appear out of thin air without any idea of where they came from, then it's time to dig back into our stories, take a fresh look and start rewriting. After all, screenplays are not carved in marble. As many screenwriters insist, screenplays are not written; they're rewritten. They exist only as words on the face of a computer terminal or scribbled on paper; therefore, we can change them at will.

William Kelley, co-writer of *Witness* (1985), states: "write and rewrite one scene until you've got it perfect, until you know the characters."[24]

Resourceful writers use a variety of techniques to bring us from Act 2 into Act 3.

EMOTIONAL TWISTS

At the end of Act 2 it may seem as if all is going well and that our protagonists have crossed to the sunny side of the street. Then a snag occurs – usually a big one – which appears to change everything.

[24] J. Wolff & K. Cox. *Top Secrets: Screenwriting.* Los Angeles: Lone Eagle. 1993.

In a love story, two lovers may have a major misunderstanding driving a wedge between them. It may take place just as they resolve seemingly irreconcilable differences. It may also be a twist in their relationship brought on by another misconception that multiplies the effect.

In *Notting Hill*, finding the boyfriend in her suite and being hounded by the media surprise us, but the writer prepares us for these possibilities so that we understand how they can happen.

The hero of the story, William, now enters Act 3 with a skewed perspective on his relationship with Anna, the movie star. He has to make decisions based on everything that happened to him.

The audience, on the other hand, wants something positive to happen. After all, as Curtis himself wrote, this is a fairy tale. And most fairy tales have happy endings.

ACTION TWISTS

Twists in story lines and plot line reversals in action stories are easier to follow - although just as hard to create effectively.

One of the clearest and most clever uses of the twist and the reversal is in *The Third Man*. Review the illustration (page 64) demonstrating how Graham Greene lays out the second act of the screenplay.

The intriguing leitmotif of the story is the character of Harry Lime. Because he is supposed to be dead, he doesn't show up until approximately two-thirds of the way through the film. A dead man comes to life – that's the first major twist in the story.

His old friend, Holly Martins, is shocked and dismayed by the sight of Lime hiding in a doorway and apparently watching out for his paramour, Anna Schmidt.

When Holly gives chase, Harry disappears. The police think Holly was drunk and discount his tale, until they discover that Harry may have disappeared into the Vienna sewers. They enter through a kiosk, where Holly sees, for the first time, the vast caverns carrying waste into the Danube.

Calloway, the police lieutenant, orders Harry's body exhumed. That's when the next twist occurs. The authorities discover that the body in Harry's coffin is that of a hospital orderly involved in Harry's blackmarket scheme.

In order to find Harry they arrest Anna. The twist in that scene occurs when we find out that she has a forged passport that Harry made for her. He rescued Anna from the Russian Zone. Now she is in danger of being sent back.

Twists and reversals plague Holly. He continues revealing his naivete when he sees Anna escorted to police headquarters:

```
                MARTINS
    I saw him buried!   And now I've
    seen him alive.
```

Calloway tries to get information from Anna, who has no knowledge of Harry except that she saw him buried. Greene gives a wonderful twist to her own view of the situation. During her interrogation two speeches indicate her feelings toward Harry as well as toward the whole sordid chase.

```
                ANNA
    I'm sorry — I don't seem able to
    understand anything you say.  He's
```

```
alive now this minute — he's doing
something.
```

Anna cares nothing about Harry's unsavory life or the wretched crimes he committed. The nature of the times - post-war Vienna, the oppression of the Soviet Union in Eastern Europe, and the seemingly amoral character of the four-power occupation forces - creates a split in Anna's thinking.

She refuses to condemn the man she once loved and who protected her, even though Anna is well aware of his criminal activities.

When Calloway insists that Harry has no chance of escape, Anna responds:

```
                ANNA
    Poor Harry, I wish he was dead, he
    would be safe from all of you then.
```

In that brief, poignant statement, we hear the anguish of a young woman talking about herself. Because she can give no information to the authorities, they have doomed her for repatriation to Soviet-controlled Czechoslovakia. The screenplay implies that she could end up in a gulag.

For Holly Martins, the biggest twist arrives when he demands that Harry's allies tell Harry that Holly wants to see him.

Over the course of Act 2, Holly's attitude changes from the uninformed tourist who arrives on a train looking for a job, to a skeptical, disappointed individual who discovers the mean truth about his one-time friend.

Act 2 of *The Third Man* rings down in an incongruous setting. Holly waits for Harry in the Russian Zone at a deserted fair ground with a circling Ferris wheel as background. Harry's arrival designates the end of Act 2. He's all smiles and an ingratiating personality.

The twists in the screenplay developed by Graham Greene and executed by the director, Carol Reed, push the audience into Act 3 with a sense of foreboding and danger lurking constantly in the background.

Greene does not create twists for shock effect. Most of them occur naturally and as part of the story. In some instances, the foreshadowing is not apparent immediately to the audience. Only in retrospect do the clues have any effect.

This represents writing with finesse and creativity. It is not necessary to slap the audience in the face every time we wish to make a point.

DISCLOSURE

Creative writing does not impart important elements by presenting them on a platter. Instead it makes each moment an unexpected unveiling so that we wish to know more, see more and understand more about the characters and the story unfolding before us.

A careful analysis of "The Big Finish" in the second act of both *Notting Hill* and *The Third Man* reveals scenes involving disclosure of secrets, feelings, and emotions that surprise and fascinate us.

The revelations in a story cannot be separated from the twists in the story. Very often they come at the same time.

In *Notting Hill* disclosures are part of the twists. The first one in Act 2 occurs when Anna tells William she will be his date at his sister's birthday party. Once we accept that piece of logic – a glamorous movie star falling for a bookstore owner, albeit a charming and handsome bookstore owner - the story can take off in many directions.

The other disclosures in the screenplay come rather rapidly in the second act. On their walk home from the birthday party, William and Anna come across one of those ubiquitous private parks that abound in London. They climb the fence and find a simple wooden bench in the garden placed there by a husband in memory of his wife of 75 years.

Anna's remark that "Some people do spend their whole lives together" discloses to us that Anna has a great longing for some kind of emotional commitment.

Later, when Anna asks William to come to her hotel suite, there's the twist of finding the ex-boyfriend, but it also discloses to us and to William that Anna has a serious problem with men who emotionally abuse her.

This revelation creates empathy for Anna and helps us understand why she has an interest in William. He's gentle, understanding, and self-effacing in an amiable, nonthreatening way.

The discovery of the ex-boyfriend comes as a shock to William who, thinking that he's been used by the movie star, tries to get on with his life. Her memory keeps intruding. After all, how does one go back to the farmer's daughter after one has touched the princess?

The next surprise comes when Anna shows up on William's doorstep. The disclosure that the press is hounding her creates the moment in which they end up making love.

That happy event is short-lived when they find the press encamped outside William's front door. Anna reveals herself as an angry, confused, and bitter young woman. Once again, William resigns himself to losing Anna. Only this time it looks permanent.

Since we have arrived at the end of Act 2, we know that there's a glimmer of hope for both of them. The fairy tale has to have a happy ending - and Curtis does not disappoint as he brings us into the third act.

FALSE HOPE

A key element in "The Big Finish" involves holding out false hope or resolving what appears to be the primary problem in the latter part of the second act.

When we resolve the primary problem, our hero or heroes look as if they have won the day, and all is well with the world. Then disaster strikes. The story often turns in new, unexpected directions, exposing the subtext.

As with most good screenplays, subtext becomes the real story. It becomes the conduit through which the theme of the screenplay flows. While the primary problem may appear obvious, the real situation may be much more subtle and dynamic.

Even though unexpected, everything that happens with our characters and our stories depends on the logic we set up at the outset. In all of the examples used so far, writers have delineated carefully who the characters are and in what kind of worlds they live.

It doesn't matter if the story is a thriller or a romance, we should not play games with the worlds we create. We should not mislead. We ought to use the rules we establish so that audiences want to see more.

When we introduce that moment of false hope into our stories, viewers have an opportunity to draw a deep breath. But if we create the proper foreshadowing, audiences will suspect that something else is afoot and be ready for it.

The solution we present in a screenplay should not be arrived at easily. Two people who fall in love have to face difficulties. Antagonists should not be defeated without a good fight.

The Subtext of *Rambling Rose*

One of the finest examples of the use of subtext shows up in Calder Willingham's screenplay based on his own novel, *Rambling Rose (1991)*.

The primary problem in the story appears to be a young woman, Rose, who disrupts an upstanding Southern family in Depression-era America. As the story proceeds and we go from one twist to another, from one revelation to another, we discover that the underlying, untold story has to do with the sexual abuse Rose suffered. For Rose, sex is the only way she knows to gain the approval of those around her.

The Subtext of *Chinatown*

Robert Towne expertly weaves his subtext into *Chinatown*. During the investigation of the death of Hollis Mulwray, Jake Gittes appears to solve part of the mystery of his inquiry. On the surface it has to do with water rights in Los Angeles.

The audience is drawn into that story only to find out that a sinister and personal story is interwoven with the plot. *Chinatown* becomes more than a political tale. A dysfunctional family and its dark secrets are the subtext of the story.

The result of an incestuous relationship years before forms the catalyst for everything that ensues in the screenplay. Therefore, all the characters – from Jake Gittes and Evelyn Mulwray to Noah Cross – must bear the burden of past.

The Subtext of *The Apostle*

In *The Apostle* (1997) written by Robert Duvall, false hope arises when, after beating a man almost to death and after fleeing from his home, The Apostle, E.F., sets up a church in a rural Louisiana town. The church flourishes. A troublemaker confronts E.F., who then converts the man.

At that point it appears as if E.F. has resolved his anger and come to terms with his own God. That moment is short-lived. Ironically, his success as an evangelical preacher draws attention, and eventually the law comes down on him. But he is now a changed man, and accepts his fate.

E.F. wants to use his power for good, but he also desires the adulation of others. He achieves both, but must pay the consequences of his prior actions.

The use of false hope or a primary resolution for *The Apostle* gives Duvall an opportunity to break through the initial premise and move into the subtext of the screenplay: how E.F. deals with his internal demons and resolves them to his own satisfaction.

That satisfaction must ring true for audiences. The resolution of the initial problem, as well as the revelation of the subtext and its outcome ought to provide them with new insights.

PUTTING IT ALL TOGETHER

Before we arrive at the door leading to Act 3, we ought to feel secure that the second act gives the audience plenty of food to chew on. Now is the time to determine whether or not we have provided a sufficiently satisfying edge - so that the audience will want to cross the threshold and continue to engage with the story and its characters.

Foreshadowing

We can utilize several techniques for accomplishing this. First of all, have we given viewers enough information or ammunition for their imaginations? By planting clues that come back, as Roberto Benigni states, like "flowers in the second part," we enable the audience to grasp the meaning of the scene. It makes sense because it does not appear out of vapor, but from a very concrete place.

The best way to accomplish this is by reading and rereading the screenplay. Determine whether or not characters or pieces of action appear because they work, and not just because they're good ideas.

Too often, new writers believe they can introduce elements into a screenplay, without giving sufficient reason, and no one will notice. It's the sure sign of not having thought through the material.

That doesn't mean that new elements cannot be written into the story. If they are, we have to go back and rewrite to ensure that they make sense when they show up.

Rewriting

The critical eye of the writer must stay focused on the needs of the story and its characters. Act 2 requires both emotional twists and twists of action in order to keep audiences on the edges of their seats. Rewriting is the key to superior screenplays. Successful writers know that their scripts must be rewritten many times before they are submitted as so-called first drafts. John Irving, who worked for thirteen years adapting his novel *Cider House Rules* (1999) for the screen, has always realized the value of rewriting. "I struggle with first drafts. I just torture myself with first drafts, and once I have a first draft, I can't revise it enough. I never tire of revising."

"I've never regretted rewriting anything. I've never regretted taking one more pass... don't be afraid of doing it because if you trust your instincts in the first place, and you make a mess of something, you'll know. You'll just know it."[25]

Twists

Emotional twists, such as those created by Richard Curtis in *Notting Hill,* usually involve individuals who come together and then are torn apart - as the result of either their own problems or outside forces that want to keep them away from one another. Those snags and those twists draw us into Act 3 because we want to see how these characters resolve their difficulties.

Action twists involve an initial danger that appears resolved but which leads to escalating danger. When it seems as if a resolution shows up in Act 2, another problem arises, thus escalating the action.

Every time we create one of those enigmas or puzzles, it should maintain the logic of the world in which it takes place in order to keep the audience focused and tuned in to the story.

---

[25] Jamie Painter. "Writing His Own Rules". *Written By:* Feb. 2000. Vol. 4, Issue 2, p. 31.

Disclosures

Disclosures or revelations based on clues or foreshadowing often become driving forces that impel the screenplay forward and push characters into unexpected directions.

When handled properly, they reveal new information about secrets in the stories, as well as the emotions and feelings of the characters involved in them. These twists play a large part in uncovering fascinating information, plot points, or knowledge about the characters.

False Hope

False hope or a false resolution to the principal problem in the story is a device meant to surprise the audience. Once that hope seems to have been reached, we discover that it's not what the story is all about. We have to jump higher hurdles blocking the crooked path ahead. When we leap over them we can find ourselves moving in new directions.

The creation of these false hopes must be based on a sense of logic and reality – whatever reality exists in the universe we create for the screenplay. Leading the audience astray for the sake of "fooling them" may work in a farce or comedy, but not in drama or melodrama. Even in comedy, we want a sense of logic to emerge. It may be skewed or off the wall, but it ought to exist so that the moment does not distract the audience.

Subtext

In "reel" life as in real life, few people expose their true agendas - unless or until they are about to go through a door one minute before they leave. Psychologists call this "exit therapy" or "door knob therapy." Patients do not reveal their true feelings until they're about to depart. That way they don't have to deal with the issues.

Subtext in a screenplay operates in much the same way. Our characters rarely reveal their true feelings. Instead they do a dance, tiptoeing around the subject and using body language (action) and words that intimate emotions and feelings. But usually they are not completely candid until they reach a critical mass – often in Act 3.

Subtext is based on the inner dynamics of the characters and the situations in which they find themselves. Characters have specific goals, and those goals may be defined by how they act. Those actions will reveal the subtext.

EXERCISES:

1. Outline the emotional and action twists in your own screenplay and how they complement each other.

2. Describe the twist at the end of Act 2 and how you pay it off in Act 3.

3. Identify the key disclosures revealed in Act 2.

4. Explain the subtext of your screenplay. If you cannot identify it, review your work and determine if it would improve by creating a subtext.

Chapter Ten
THE WHOLE STORY

The purpose of storytelling is to draw the audience into the tale and provide insights into the characters who propel our story.

For the audience to experience a feeling of satisfaction, the center of the screenplay - the core of the story where action, conflict, and tension take place, - must contain all the necessary elements. The logical ending we choose out of the multiple resolutions possible must seem as if it's the only one that makes sense.

STRUCTURE

When we review the last act of *The Third Man*, it shocks us to find out that the ultimate executioner of Harry Lime is his best friend, a man who throughout the story comes off as a naif. But he gains in knowledge and stature throughout Act 2, so that, while Holly's final move disturbs us, it also comes off as believable, since the killing represents a justifiable act as well as an act of mercy.

The screenplay supplies abundant twists and turns, revelations, false hopes, and disclosures with a strong subtext. It helps us understand Holly Martins' motivations; Anna Schmidt's reasons for acting as she does; as well as the dogged persistence of Calloway, the British security agent.

Graham Greene prepares the setting for us at the very beginning of the screenplay when the narrator intones: "I never knew the old Vienna before the war, with its Strauss music, its glamour and easy charm... I really got to know it in the classic period of the black market. We'd run anything if people wanted it enough. And had the money to pay. Of course a situation like that doesn't tempt ama-

141

teurs... You know, they can't stay the course like a professional."
Over the last line we see a corpse floating in the Danube River.

The second act of *The Third Man* opens with the revelation that a
third man witnessed the death of Harry Lime. The writer builds
one incident on another with precision and logic. The devious and
convoluted story carries us along because we have an investment in
the characters and their dilemmas.

Without the heightened melodrama and sense of danger lurking
around every corner of the screenplay, we would have no interest in
crossing into the third act for the exciting conclusion of the film.

In *Shakespeare In Love*, Act 3 culminates with the completion of the
play Romeo and Juliet. Everything that occurs in Act 2 leads to that
moment onstage even though the lovers, Will and Viola, will separate. They die a figurative death, while the characters in the play die
a literal death.

The story developed by Marc Norman and Tom Stoppard parallels
that of the fictional play written by William Shakespeare. The inge-
nious concept is that the love story between the playwright and his
ladylove becomes Shakespeare's inspiration to continue writing.

The parallels are deliberate, even though a viewer would have to
know the plays of Shakespeare, as well as have some knowledge of
the times in which he wrote to grasp all the inside jokes, innuendoes,
and pieces of action. An example is the first time Will sees Viola as
herself. The scene description in the screenplay reads:

"The guests form up to begin a changing-partners dance (the very
same one you get in every ROMEO AND JULIET)."[26]

However, Marc Norman explains: "...I never wanted the audience to

[26] Marc Norman & Tom Stoppard. Op. cit. New York: Miramax Books. 1998. p. 42

need to know about Shakespeare in order to enjoy the movie. When I was writing it, I kept on envisioning an inner-city kid watching the movie, and I kept saying to myself, 'Is he getting it?'"[27]

The two lovers come from opposite sides of the social fence: she from nobility and he from a merchant family in the small town of Stratford-on-Avon. As in the Shakespeare play, the young woman in the screenplay, Viola, has been promised in marriage to another. She is not happy about her betrothal to a man she loathes. Just as in *Romeo and Juliet*, disguises play a large part in the deceit between lovers.

Will needs a muse to help him overcome his writer's block. On the other hand, Viola, angered over her betrothal and with a rather liberated outlook on life, has fallen in love with the theater at a time when the law forbids women from appearing onstage.

All of these elements come together as they create conflict and tension in Act 2 of *Shakespeare In Love*. The writers carefully craft a romantic comedy that builds relationships filled with emotions and feelings.

Many of the characters in Norman and Stoppard's script are mirror images of the characters in Shakespeare's drama - from the Nurse to Wessex (Paris in the play), to Viola's parents the de Lesseps (the Capulets).

The bawdy humor and many of the lively moments, such as the balcony scene, correspond to scenes in the play. If we know *Romeo and Juliet*, then we expect Act 3 to end as it does. If we do not know the play, then all the events, crises, twists, revelations, and false hopes make the ending one that we can accept readily.

---

[27] Susan Billington Katz. "A Conversation with Marc Norman and Tom Stoppard: Rhyme or Reason". *Written By:* March 1999. Vol. 3, Issue 3, p. 21.

Both of these screenplays, Greene in his classic vintage thriller and Norman and Stoppard in their contemporary 17-th century romantic comedy, bring the conflict to a new peak in the second act.

The Third Man operates within the confines of the classic "innocent man thrust into danger" situation. However, it twists the story in such a way that the formula feels fresh even by today's standards. Although Holly Martins appears to be the main character, Harry Lime dominates the story, though he does not appear until the last third of the film.

Holly's character changes from a trusting naive person to a skeptical and disappointed one as the film progresses. Harry's character changes depending on who describes him. It isn't until we meet him that we see him as an ingratiatingly dangerous sociopath.

Shakespeare In Love carries with it the notion of opposites. The main characters, Will and Viola, want something they cannot have. Will desires Viola, a young woman of noble birth. But as we discover, he has a wife and children back in Stratford-on-Avon. Even if he were not married, he comes from the newly emerging middle class. Marriage between the classes rarely takes place.

Viola initially wants to be in the theater, but the authorities do not allow females onstage. She disguises herself as a boy, auditions at the Rose Theater, and falls in love with the poetry - as well as with the young man who writes the words, Will Shakespeare.

These are all the ingredients necessary for the clashing of classes, the conflict of interests, tension between lovers, and emotional fallout - all cooked up so that the audience will have a personal investment in the story.

CHARACTER AND STORY MOTIVATION

The successful resolution of a screenplay relies primarily on the motivation behind the characters. We have to understand why they have become involved in the adventure.

Characters should not ride on the back of the story. They must have a persevering need to become integrated into the screenplay so that neither the story nor the characters can separate one from the other. If we can achieve that, then we have come a long way in developing a film story that holds the audience's fascination.

Without Jake Gittes *Chinatown* would become a different story. His backstory, although hidden for the most part, emerges in bits and pieces throughout the screenplay.

The first scene depicts him as a cool detective who appears to operate on the surface. As Towne moves deeper into the story, he reveals Gittes as someone with a much more profound sense of right and wrong, eager to see justice done.

Towne uses the Depression effectively in a scene between Gittes and a barbershop customer, who happens to be a loan officer at a local bank. It permits us to get a sense of the time in which the story takes place, as well as take a peek into the detective's moral underpinnings. The customer complains about a news story concerning Gittes being hired by a wealthy woman. Gittes responds:

```
                    GITTES
          Look, pal — I make an honest living.
          People don't come to me unless
          they're miserable and I help 'em out
          of bad situations.  I don't kick them
```

145

> out of their homes like you jerks who
> work in the bank.

Later, when Gittes shows up where a body has been found, we discover that he had once been on the police force. This piece of information eliminates the need to explain the way he operates and the people he knows.

Further on in the second act, Towne creates another revelation when Gittes says: "It's what the DA used to tell me about Chinatown." Now we know he operated out of the District Attorney's office. Our curiosity deepens. We want to know more. What pushed him out of the D.A.'s office?

Each of these moments provide motivation for the protagonist.

When he acts and reacts, we understand where he comes from and why he behaves the way he does.

Every revelatory scene drives the story forward. While the scene with the barbershop customer gives us a sense of Gittes hanging in there for the underdog, it also furnishes an opportunity to explore the newspaper stories reporting Hollis Mulwray's infidelities and Gittes' involvement as the detective on the case. The story turns into one with citywide interest. The subtext of the scene takes place offscreen. We hear other customers talking about the drought in Los Angeles.

Several story points are made in the scene between Noah Cross and Jake Gittes in the middle of the second act. After Cross warns the detective about taking on his daughter's case, Gittes retorts with the remark about the D.A.'s warning.

On the one hand we see the diabolical nature of Cross. On the other hand, we see that Gittes does not scare easily. The more warnings he receives, the more likely he will become driven to find answers. At that juncture, when the protagonist beards the lion in his den, the story takes a leap forward into the latter half of the second act.

Robert Duvall's *The Apostle* draws us in because of the unique nature of the protagonist, E.F. In some ways he represents an anti-hero, a man filled with so many flaws that, while we want him to succeed, we also want him to get hold of himself and straighten out his life. In a sense, he makes us pray for him.

Near the end of Act 1, Sonny, (E.F.), stands by himself in his room and screams out his frustration with God. His wife has left him and taken his two children. He can't understand the source of his tribulations and wants a sign from heaven to tell him why.

The complex nature of his personality continues to emerge throughout the screenplay. Sonny, or E.F., or, as he comes to be called in the second act of the story, The Apostle, finds himself drawn to a religious calling. And this from a man who has demonstrated a wild, violent nature.

Act 1 reveals his violent nature when he batters his wife's boyfriend. It becomes the inciting incident for him to run, moving the screenplay into the second act.

Story and character meld into one. E.F. wanders deep into the bayou country of Louisiana. His life at that point is summed up in one line of dialogue: "So I reckon you would know what it means to face the possibility of losing everybody and everything?"[28]

The sparse nature of the revelations that occur in *The Apostle* go a long way toward an understanding of the poetry of the screenplay.

---

[28] Robert Duvall. *The Apostle*. New York: October/Boulevard Books. 1997. p. 40.

Duvall explains E.F. and his attraction to black gospel preaching by providing several brief expository scenes. In one scene, E.F. reminisces about a time when he was five years old and taken by his black nanny to a country church to hear a black preacher. The scene has no dialogue. However, the implication becomes very clear. The church, the preacher, and the gospel music have a profound impact on the child.

The screenwriter permits the audience to interpret the dialogue and the action in terms of the story and the character's direction.

Later in the second act, E.F. helps a man injured on the job. The scene is a replay of an incident in the first act, when he ministers to a man injured in an automobile accident. In both scenes he's warned to keep away: in the factory by his boss and in the accident by a police officer. In both cases he continues out of conviction.

Now we begin to see the value of E.F.'s violent nature set against his religious calling. The fervor inherent in his preaching, the passion imbued in his words, the spirit that keeps him going could not exist without his underlying anger.

E.F.'s determination remains strong because he will not depart from the path he has chosen. In the latter part of Act 2 he makes a statement that sums up his whole personality: "No one is going to paralyze any dream of mine." [29]

INTO ACT 3

One of the keys to the success of these screenplays is how effectively they draw the audience into the third act. Writers should bring conflicts to new peaks, beyond the places we expect them to go.

In the second act of *The Third Man*, after following the protagonist

[29] Ibid. p. 96.

148

on his quest to clear his friend's name, and while he has been pursued by killers, the big shock is the appearance of the friend we assumed had been dead and buried.

In the first scene of Act 3, we discover more about Harry and Holly's relationship. Holly, always concerned about other people, reports that the British plan to hand Anna, Harry's girlfriend, over to the Russians for deportation. In a strange piece of action, Harry draws a heart with the letters "H" and "A" on the window of the Ferris wheel gondola – the action of a young man carving a heart on a tree. Then he responds cynically: "What can I do, old man, I'm dead, aren't I?"[30]

The shock of seeing the supposed dead man alive, and the new revelations that propel the story forward, make it imperative for us to want to know how Holly will resolve his moral dilemmas. One dilemma has to do with Harry's illegal activities and the harm they have done to society. Another dilemma involves his long friendship with Harry. And the third dilemma encompasses his relationship with Anna.

Having all of these converge at the end of Act 2 and the beginning of Act 3 intensifies the emotional payoff for the audience as well as the characters. Graham Greene cleverly raises the ante so that we jump into the third act eagerly awaiting a conclusion that both satisfies and surprises us.

Shakespeare In Love creates wonderful tension at the end of Act 2 by emulating *Romeo and Juliet*. In trying to escape from Wessex, the man promised to Viola, Will lies. He tells Wessex he is Christopher Marlowe, another writer.

Act 2 ends with the news that Marlowe has been murdered. The assumption Will makes is that Wessex is the assassin. Act 3 begins

---

[30] Graham Greene. Op.cit.

with Viola hearing the news that the "playwright" has been killed. At this point, those who know *Romeo and Juliet* could assume that she will follow Juliet's fate. The difference, since this is a romantic comedy, comes immediately when Will shows up.

The question still remains: How will Viola and Will work out their relationship? Viola answers that she must marry Wessex at the Queen's command. However she promises Will: "...I will go to Wessex as a widow from these vows, as solemn as they are unsanctified."[31]

Act 3 is the culmination of all that has gone on before. Marc Norman and Tom Stoppard draw us into the climax and conclusion - with death threats, sword fights, Viola's urgent need to act onstage, and, in the end, her role as William Shakespeare's muse. Viola inspires him to write his great comedy *Twelfth Night*, whose heroine he names Viola.

The scenes leading up to Act 3 in *Chinatown* reveal the subtext of Jake Gittes' personality. These scenes were explored in previous chapters. However, it's important to look once more to see how Robert Towne uses them to thrust the story forward.

Gittes admits that while working in the District Attorney's office, he hurt someone even though he was trying to help.

His vulnerability exposed throughout Act 2 leads Evelyn Mulwray, the widow of the man whose murder he investigates, to take him to her home. They make love and their relationship appears on the move - until she receives a strange phone call. That call and Gittes' suspicions crack open the very personal, dysfunctional subtext of the screenplay. The audience gets hooked and wants to hold on for the remainder of the ride.

---

[31] Marc Norman & Tom Stoppard. Op. cit. p. 113.

Act 2 of *The Apostle* delves into the interior life of the main character, E.F. Robert Duvall's screenplay takes us into the hell of one man's redemption by showing us various facets of his personality. Because the complexity of the protagonist mirrors the complexity audiences see within themselves and others, the story becomes personal.

Everyone wears different masks at different times in their lives, and often at different times during the day. We are mothers, fathers, brothers, sisters, sons, daughters, bosses, underlings, teachers, and students. Our relationships change according to the position we hold at a particular time.

Duvall creates the same kind of multifaceted character with E.F. In Act 1, when he clubs a man to death, he calls himself "Sonny." Then as he makes the decision to build a church and preach, he names himself "E.F." (His real name is Euliss F. Dewey.) When he reaches the apex of preaching, he calls himself "The Apostle."

Confused by his own crisis of identity he asks Blackwell, the black co-pastor of his church, "What do you want me to do?"[32]

The next scene takes us into Act 3. His wife, Jessie, hears E.F. preaching on the radio. The spiral taking the story to its conclusion begins. It culminates in a rip-roaring Evangelical sermon followed by his resignation to the police, who arrest him.

The screenplay has elements of myth and folktale blended together. In his anger, E.F., emulates Jesus when he confronts the moneychangers and others who prey on humanity. His determined way of raising money and building the church raise him to almost mythic proportions on Pecan Island, Louisiana, where he reaches the status of a hero.

His arrest becomes a metaphor for the need to pay for wrongdoing

[32] Robert Duvall. Op. cit. p. 114.

as one step on the road to his own redemption. At the moment of his arrest he reconciles himself: "I'm an Apostle for our Lord now. I'm the man you're looking for."[33]

By creating these dramatic moments, all of which build on one another seamlessly, the writers develop stories that resonate with their audiences. The motion pictures draw us into their stories because we need to know the solutions to the problems presented.

PUTTING IT ALL TOGETHER

The screenplays discussed in this chapter fall into a variety of genres: mystery (*The Third Man*), romantic-comedy (*Shakespeare In Love*), vengeance-mystery (*Chinatown*), and personal quest (*The Apostle*).

However, they have features in common that take them out of the ordinary and place them in that rarified atmosphere of motion pictures which have found their way into our cultural mythology.

All four films are character-driven. The characters push and pull the stories along with them. They do not exist for the purpose of riding along and giving the writer an excuse for creating dialogue. Their dialogue, action, and motivations provide the substance of the screenplay as well as the underlying subtext.

Within the structure of each of the screenplays we can find several paradigms that work effectively.

The Third Man emulates the hero's journey - by taking a person out of ordinary circumstances and pushing him into the hero's role. He must use his wits and wile to discover the truth and return with some kind of reward. The story, however, does not completely fulfill that formula. The reward comes in the form of clearing his friend's name as well as his failed attempt to obtain the love of a woman.

---

[33] Ibid. p. 127.

The theory of opposites functions in *Shakespeare In Love*. Both hero and heroine want something they cannot have: each other. They go after it with all their energy. They achieve unseen goals by having a love affair that transcends their present life. A great play is created based on that affair. A woman accomplishes something no one had ever done at that time: appearing on an Elizabethan stage.

Chinatown presents itself as a puzzle, in which the detective, as the outsider, has to find the missing pieces in order to solve the mystery. The more he delves into the mystery, the more he becomes involved in the lives of other people. Because of the nature of his personality, a man who fights for the underdog, he becomes intertwined with both the puzzle and the mystery, so that he has a deep personal investment in solving the riddle.

Robert Duvall's journey of discovery in *The Apostle* leads the protagonist down a road of self-revelation. Character is the story. It presents a complex individual who needs to explode outwardly as well as inwardly in order to achieve his own sense of grace. The life trip the character takes is akin to a religious pilgrimage, and similar to how religious personalities of the past often emerged from ordinary, often disreputable backgrounds.

Aristotle in his *Poetics* wrote in the third century BCE: "A whole is that which has a beginning, middle, and end." [34]

In reality, no formula exists for creating great stories. Everything depends upon the creators. A good beginning requires an excellent middle in order to achieve a satisfying end.

[34] Aristotle. *Poetics*. New York: Hill & Wang 1989.

EXERCISES:

1. Review the structure of your screenplay.

    A. Briefly describe how you set up the conflict.
    B. Identify how you create conflict and tension.
    C. Indicate how you resolve the conflict.

2. Analyze the key motivations behind your protagonist and your antagonist.

REFERENCED FILMS AND THEIR WRITERS

AFFLICTION (1997) Writer: Paul Schrader. Novel: Russell Banks.

THE APOSTLE (1997) Writer: Robert Duvall.

THE BIG NIGHT (1996) Writers: Stanley Tucci, Campbell Scott.

BRAVEHEART (1995) Writer: Randall Wallace.

CHINATOWN (1974) Writer: Robert Towne.

CIDER HOUSE RULES (1999) Writer: John Irving. Novel: John Irving.

ENEMY OF THE STATE (1998) Writer: David Marconi.

THE ENGLISH PATIENT (1997) Writer: Anthony Minghella.

IN THE LINE OF FIRE (1993) Writer: Jeff Maguire.

JOE GOULD'S SECRET (2000) Writers: Stanley Tucci, Howard Rodman. Novel: Joseph Mitchell.

LIFE IS BEAUTIFUL (1998) Writers: Roberto Benigni, Vincenzo Cerami.

MISSION IMPOSSIBLE (1998) Writers: David Koepp, Robert Towne. Story: David Koepp, Steve Zaillian. Based on the TV series created by Bruce Geller.

MISSION IMPOSSIBLE 2 (2000) Writer: Robert Towne. Story: Ronald D. Moore, Brannon Braga. Based on the TV series created by Bruce Geller.

THE MUSE (1999) Writer: Albert Brooks.

NORTH BY NORTHWEST (1959) Writer: Ernest Lehman.

NOTTING HILL (1999) Writer: Richard Curtis.

PRINCE OF EGYPT (1999) Writers: Philip LaZebnik, Nicholas Meyer.

RAMBLING ROSE (1991) Writer: Calder Willingham.

SHAKESPEARE IN LOVE (1999) Writers: Marc Norman, Tom Stoppard.

SILENCE OF THE LAMBS (1990) Writer: Ted Tally. Novel: Thomas Harris.

SPITFIRE GRILL (1996) Writer: David Zlotoff.

THE SWEET HEREAFTER (1997) Writer: Atom Egoyan. Novel: Russell Banks.

THE TALENTED MR. RIPLEY (1999) Writer: Anthony Minghella. Novel: Patricia Highsmith.

TERMINATOR (1984) Writers: James Cameron, Gale Anne Hurd.

THE THIRD MAN (1949) Writer: Graham Greene.

THREE DAYS OF THE CONDOR (1975) Writers: Lorenzo Semple, Jr., David Rayfield. Novel: *Seven Days of the Condor* by James Grady.

TOPKAPI (1964) Writer: Monja Danishewsky. Novel: *The Light of Day* by Eric Ambler.

WHEN HARRY MET SALLY... (1989) Writer: Nora Ephron.

YOU'VE GOT MAIL (1998) Writers: Miklos Laszlo, Nora Ephron, Delia Ephron. Based on the screenplay *The Shop Around the Corner* (1940) by Samson Raphaelson.

THE WRITER'S LIBRARY

These are books all writers should have in their libraries. Keep them close at hand – preferably right near your work place. That way you can refer to them without having to search your bookcases – or boot up an Internet site. Of course, if you're into avoidance behavior, searching for those books provides a good excuse. Whenever someone wants to know what you're doing you can always say you're doing research.

(Almost all of these books and research materials can now be found on the Internet)

Roget's International Thesaurus
American Heritage Dictionary
Oxford Dictionary
Bulfinch's Mythology
Grimm's Fairy Tales (the complete works)
The Bible
Travel books (AAA, Michelin Guides, etc.)

THE WEB

Specialty Search Engines

www.britannica.com (Encyclopaedia Britannica)

www.encyclopedia.com (another online encyclopedia)

www.thepaperboy.com (searches over 2,500 online newspapers)

Fast Facts

www.ipl.org/ref (Internet Public Library with general references and subcategories)

thorplus.lib.purdue.edu/reference/index.html (Purdue University's library website. Lists all kinds of reference books by category)

www.itools.com/research-it/research-it.html (a direct research site with multiple options)

www.odic.gov/cia/publications/factbook/index.html (a genuine CIA website with worldwide facts only that organization would gather together)

MICHAEL HALPERIN

Michael Halperin teaches screenwriting and broadcasting at Loyola Marymount University in Los Angeles, California, and a writing seminar at the American Film Institute. He also teaches screenwriting seminars in UCLA's Writers Program.

He worked on staff at Universal, and was Executive Story Consultant for 20th Century Fox Television. He has written for popular television shows such as *Star Trek: The Next Generation*, *Falcon Crest*, and *Quincy*. He was the Creative Consultant and wrote the Bible for one of television's most successful animated series, *Masters of the Universe*.

Halperin is co-author of the best-selling novel for children, *Jacob's Rescue*, as well as the author of *Writing Great Characters*, a book for writers adopted by universities around the nation. His play *The Spark of Reason* was produced recently in Los Angeles.

He has written, designed, and produced several best-selling computer-based interactive media programs and won the "Cybie" award from the Academy of Interactive Arts & Sciences as co-writer of *Voyeur*, one of the first interactive murder-mysteries.

He holds a BA degree in Communications from USC and a Ph.D. in Film Studies.

Photo by: Leon Halperin

SEMINARS WITH
MICHAEL HALPERIN

SEMINARS WITH
MICHAEL HALPERIN

For a dynamic, inspirational encounter,

arrange for a one or two day seminar

with Michael Halperin on

Character Development

and Screenwriting

Michael Halperin also provides literary

consulting services to help you develop

strong characters, insightful concepts

and well-crafted stories that have impact.

Rates upon request

Michael Halperin
818.907.6281
818.788.2725 (Fax)
e-mail: michaelhalperin@sprintmail.com

Screenwriting 101
The Essential Craft of Feature Film Writing

Neill D. Hicks

Hicks, a successful screenwriter whose credits include *Rumble in the Bronx* and *First Strike*, brings the clarity and practical instruction familiar to his UCLA students to screenwriters everywhere. In his refreshingly straightforward style, Hicks tells the beginning screenwriter how the mechanics of Hollywood storytelling work, and how to use those elements to create a script with blockbuster potential without falling into cliches. Also discussed are the practicalities of the business—securing an agent, pitching your script, protecting your work, and other topics essential to building a career in screenwriting.

"Neill Hicks makes complex writing concepts easy to grasp, in a way that only a master teacher could. And he does so while keeping his book one hell of a fun read."
Eric Edson, Screenwriter and Executive Director of the Hollywood Symposium

NEILL HICKS is a professional screenwriter and a senior instructor at the UCLA Extension Writer's Program, where he has been honored with the Outstanding Instructor Award. He has also taught graduate courses on screenwriting at the University of Denver, presented a seminar on Selling to Hollywood at the Denver International Film Festival, and conducts screenwriting workshops throughout the United States, Canada, and Europe. Visit his Web site at **www.screenwriting101.net**.

Movie Entertainment Book Club Selection
Doubleday Stage and Screen Selection

$16.95, ISBN 0-941188-72-8
220 pages, 6 x 9
Order # 41RLS

The Writer's Journey
—2nd Edition
Mythic Structure for Writers

Christopher Vogler

THE WRITER'S JOURNEY
2ND EDITION
MYTHIC STRUCTURE FOR WRITERS

CHRISTOPHER VOGLER

See why this book has become an international best seller, and a true classic. First published in 1992, *The Writer's Journey* explores the powerful relationship between mythology and storytelling in a clear, concise style that's made it required reading for movie executives, screenwriters, scholars, and lovers of pop culture all over the world.

Writers of both fiction and non-fiction will discover a set of useful myth-inspired storytelling paradigms (i.e. *The Hero's Journey*) and step-by-step guidelines to plot and character development. Based on the work of Joseph Campbell, *The Writer's Journey* is a must for writers of all kinds interested in further developing their craft.

The updated and revised 2nd edition provides new insights and observations from Vogler's ongoing work on mythology's influence on stories, movies, and man himself.

> "This is a book about the stories we write, and perhaps more importantly, the stories we live. It is the most influential work I have yet encountered on the art, nature, and the very purpose of storytelling."
> **Bruce Joel Rubin**, Screenwriter, *Ghost, Jacob's Ladder*

Book of the Month Club Selection • Writer's Digest Book Club Selection • Movie Entertainment Book Club Selection • Doubleday Stage and Screen Selection

CHRIS VOGLER has been a top Hollywood story consultant and development executive for over 15 years. He has worked on such top grossing feature films as *The Thin Red Line*, *Fight Club*, *The Lion King*, and *Beauty and the Beast*. His international workshops have taken him to Germany, Italy, United Kingdom and Spain, and his literary consulting service Storytech provides in-depth evaluations for professional writers. To learn more, visit his Web site at **www.thewritersjourney.com**.

$22.95, ISBN 0-941188-70-1
300 pages, 6 x 9
Order # 98RLS

Myth & the Movies

Discovering the Mythic Structure of 50 Unforgettable Films

Stuart Voytilla

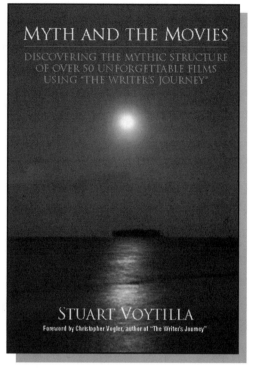

Foreword by **Christopher Vogler**, author of "The Writer's Journey"

With this collection of essays exploring the mythic structure of 50 well-loved U.S. and foreign films, Voytilla has created a fun and fascinating book for film fans, screenwriters, and anyone with a love of storytelling and pop culture.

An informal companion piece to the best-selling *The Writer's Journey* by Christopher Vogler, *Myth and the Movies* applies the mythic structure Vogler developed to films as diverse as "Die Hard," "Singin' in the Rain" and "Boyz N the Hood." This comprehensive book offers a greater understanding of why some films continue to touch and connect with audiences generation after generation.

Movies discussed include *Annie Hall, Beauty and the Beast, Chinatown, Citizen Kane, E.T., The Fugitive, The Godfather, The Graduate, La Strada, The Piano, Pulp Fiction, Notorious, Raiders of the Lost Ark, The Searchers, The Silence of the Lambs, T2–Judgment Day, Sleepless in Seattle, Star Wars, Unforgiven,* and many more.

STUART VOYTILLA is a writer, script consultant, and teacher of acting and screenwriting. He has evaluated hundreds of scripts for LA -based talent agencies. His latest screenplay, *The Golem*, is being produced by Baltimore-based Princess Pictures.

Movie Entertainment Book Club Selection

$26.95, ISBN 0-941188-66-3
300 pages, 7 x 10, illustrations throughout
Order # 39RLS

MICHAEL WIESE PRODUCTIONS

11288 Ventura Blvd., Suite 821
Studio City, CA 91604
1-818-379-8799
kenlee@earthlink.net
www.mwp.com

Write or Fax
for a
free catalog.

Please send me the following books:

Title   Order Number (#RLS___)   Amount

_____ _____

_____ _____

_____ _____

_____ _____

SHIPPING   _____

California Tax (8.25%)   _____

TOTAL ENCLOSED _____

Please make check or money order payable to
Michael Wiese Productions

(Check one) ____ Master Card ___Visa ____Amex

Credit Card Number_____

Expiration Date_____

Cardholder's Name_____

Cardholder's Signature_____

SHIP TO:

Name_____

Address_____

City_____State_____Zip_____